Quit Going
to Church

Quit Going
to Church

Bob Hostetler

LEAFWOOD
PUBLISHERS

QUIT GOING TO CHURCH

Copyright 2012 by Bob Hostetler

ISBN 978-0-915547-70-8
LCCN 2011047190

Printed in the United States of America

LIBRARY OF CONGRESS CATALOGING-IN-PUBLICATION DATA
Hostetler, Bob, 1958-
Quit going to church / by Robert Hostetler.
    p. cm.
ISBN 978-0-915547-70-8
1. Christian life. I. Title.
BV4501.3.H678 2012
248.4--dc23

                                                                        2011047190

Cover design by Marc Whitaker
Interior text design by Sandy Armstrong

Cover photo of timecard machine courtesy of Doug Webb

Leafwood Publishers is an imprint of
Abilene Christian University Press
1626 Campus Court
Abilene, Texas 79601

1-877-816-4455
www.leafwoodpublishers.com

12 13 14 15 16 17 / 7 6 5 4 3 2 1

Dedicated to

The Salvation Army,
to whom, as individuals and as a whole,
I owe much.

Acknowledgments

Thank you to Steve Laube of the Steve Laube Agency for representing me on this project.

Thank you to Dr. Leonard Allen, Gary Myers, Robyn Burwell, and all the folks at Leafwood Publishers for believing in this book and its message, and for the expertise that made it better at every point in the process.

Thank you to the many thinkers, writers, and influencers who helped shape the concepts and perspectives offered in this book: my parents Millie and Vernon, my brothers Don and Larry, William and Catherine Booth, Samuel Logan Brengle, Eugene Peterson, Marva Dawn, Mike Erre, Erwin McManus, Annie Dillard, Phyllis Tickle, John Johnson, Thomas Merton and the brothers of the Abbey of Gethsemani, John Ortberg, Brian McLaren, Andy Stanley, Philip Yancey, Michael Spencer, Shane Claiborne, Rob Bell, Steve McVey, C. S. Lewis, Peter Marshall, Rick Warren, N. T. Wright, Brennan Manning, Tim Stafford, and the leaders and members of Cobblestone Community Church, among others.

Thank you to Major Raphael Jackson, Major Bill Bender, and Tony Campolo for the permission to mine their memories and experiences for the message of this book.

Thank you also to Barbara Johnson, Cheryl Johnson, Julie Sellers, Scott Sellers, Deb Smith, Gary Smith, Debbie Stumph, Steve Stumph, Doug Webb, and Julie Webb for their prayer efforts on behalf of this book, throughout the writing and editing process.

Thank you also—and most of all—to the lovely Robin, my wife, without whose love and support I could not have begun, let alone finish, this project.

Table of Contents

Introduction

George MacDonald's novel *The Curate's Awakening* contains a scene in which a pastor is talking to a man who is thoroughly skeptical toward the Christian faith. MacDonald, a masterful nineteenth-century novelist (and clergyman himself), depicts the skeptic accusing the churchgoing people of the community with the words, "Just because there's a church standing somewhere doesn't necessarily mean there's faith inside its walls. . . . Their so-called religion does them no good. They don't really believe everything they say, or what they hear from the pulpit. They fill up the churches every Sunday, but as I said before, there's no faith."

The pastor objects, of course, and insists that this is an unfair characterization. But the skeptic continues. "I assert that the form of Christianity commonly practiced [by you, and] by most of the rest of your congregation, comes nearer the views of the heathen poet Horace than those of your saint, the old Jew, Saul of Tarsus."[1]

Well, of course, the pastor thinks the man is wrong. At first. However, as the story continues, the pastor honestly confronts the possibility that the skeptic may have been right.

What if we did that? What if we stopped to consider the skeptic's words? We know, of course, that much of what goes on in our churches (and in our Christian lives) is the result of adaptation and accommodation . . . even improvement. In most cases, that's neither here nor there. Jesus never sang hymns to the accompaniment of an organ . . . or a guitar, but we know he sang hymns.[2] The Apostle Paul never excerpted a movie in any of his sermons, but he did quote pagan poets.[3] We don't even have records of the early followers of Jesus meeting in church buildings, let alone structures with steeples or pulpits or media projection screens.

And the church is changing rapidly, and drastically, in some places. Recent decades have seen the introduction (in some churches) of coffee cups into church sanctuaries, guitars and drums into church music, and animated vegetables into church teaching. Not only are some churches "traditional" and others "contemporary," but some are "seeker-sensitive" and others are "emergent." Some are "multicultural" and others are "multi-site."

But most of us aren't bothered by those kinds of differences between the way of Jesus and the way we practice the "faith that was once for all entrusted to the saints."[4] We have no trouble admitting that we have adapted or updated the way we "do church," because we live in a different day and age than the first Christians did.

But what if we've done more than that? What if the form of Christianity commonly practiced by us and by most of the Christians around us bears little—if any—resemblance to the way of Jesus and the kingdom he came to earth to usher in? What if we've missed the boat in more important things, like how to talk to God and how to please him? What if we've misunderstood—even misrepresented—what it means to truly follow Jesus?

The late Michael Spencer, also known as the Internet Monk, wrote the following in his book, *Mere Churchianity*:

> Our big problem with Jesus is that we want to control things, and he turns out to be remarkably difficult to control. In the Christian enterprise, we like to formulate definitions, establish norms, and set parameters for acceptable experiences. We have empowered ourselves to determine what is and is not an appropriate relationship with Jesus, based on how we think Christianity should look and work. . . . Would Jesus recognize the church of twenty-first century North America as the movement he began? I'm not interested in how the youth program introduces people to Jesus or how the Easter pageant represented the last days of Christ. I want to know what would happen if Jesus paid a quality-control visit. Would he recognize this movement, as we've reconstructed it, as bearing any resemblance to what he began in those forty days post-resurrection and beyond?[5]

That's what this book is about: identifying and correcting the ways we have forgotten—or departed from—the way of Jesus. It's a journey I hope we can take together, an exploration I hope we can undertake as partners. Along the way, I imagine we're going to ruffle more than a few feathers. At times, the going will get really hard, and we're going to be challenged and stretched, turned upside down, and maybe even broken.

But I pray that, when I am done writing and when you are done reading, together we will be more in love with God than ever before and more active in bringing his kingdom in and throughout our communities.

Amen.

CHAPTER ONE

Quit Going to Church

I have been going to church since I was two or three weeks old. Not that I remember it, but I'm told that my parents, Vernon and Millie, bundled me up and carried me in to the little downtown church we attended as a family. My two older brothers were there, too, and I was reasonably well-behaved. I didn't sing when everyone else sang, and I didn't pay much attention to the sermon, but at least I didn't crawl under the seats and tie people's shoestrings together or anything like that. There would be time enough for that later on in life.

When I was old enough, I started attending "children's church" while my older brothers and parents were going to "grownups' church." I had my first encounter with the living Christ there while kneeling at an old wooden altar (which had once been used in grownups' church, but when they got a new altar for some reason—maybe they needed pads for their grownup knees—the children's ministry got their hand-me-down altar).

That's one of my earliest memories, in fact: confessing my sins and asking Jesus to take up residence in my four- or five-year-old heart, which he did. I know because he has had to remind me often since that day.

But I didn't just go to church on Sunday mornings. No, my family members were not just Sunday-morning Christians, like some less-consecrated folks. After a rather full Sunday morning that involved serving breakfast to the homeless (along with a short evangelistic service, which my parents often led) and attending age-appropriate Sunday school classes followed by children's church (for me) and grownups' church for my brothers and parents, we would return home for the afternoon before making the half-hour drive downtown again on Sunday evening for another church service. Not to mention (but I will) midweek prayer meetings or practices or Bible studies that grossly hindered my ability to keep culturally current with *Patty Duke, The Rifleman, Shindig!,* and *Hullabaloo.*

I estimate that I have gone to church more than five thousand times in my life. I can't remember a single time in my childhood or teen years when I stayed home from church. (I can remember trying nearly every trick in the book to stay home some Sundays; I learned at an early age, however, that neither stomachache nor headache nor severe hallucinations would work on my mom.) For most of my life, I attended two or more church services a week. As an adult, even including family vacations, I can count the number of times I have *not* gone to church on the fingers of both hands, or maybe on just one (though I suppose this record is tempered somewhat by the fact that for roughly twenty years I have been a pastor . . . but it still oughta count, right?).

Nonetheless, despite all that history and experience, I believe I can act as God's representative, speaking in Jesus' name, when I urge you to *quit going to church.*

Going through a Phrase

"Going to church."

Take a minute to think of how we use that phrase.

When we think or speak of going to church, we use the word *church* to refer to an event. An occasion. A denomination, perhaps. Or a place: a specific building or location.

Yet you will never find that concept, that terminology, that way of thinking in the Bible.

It's not there.

It's utterly foreign to what the Bible means when it talks about the "church."

Of all the parables Jesus told, he never told a story about people going to church—not the way we do today. Of all the things he taught his disciples, as far as we know, he never taught them anything on the subject of going to church. In all he said, he never commanded church attendance.

So I'd like to suggest that, even if you don't think you can join me in *resigning* from that way of thinking (and the way of behaving that goes along with it) and quit "going to church," you at least keep an open mind for the next few pages. I'll try to show how in this area, as in a great many others, a whole lot of how we think and act, a great percentage of what we do these days as churchgoing people, bears only a slight resemblance to the way of Jesus and "the faith that was once for all entrusted to the saints," as the Bible says in Jude 1:3.

An Early Church Snapshot

The book of Acts—the fifth book of the New Testament—is an account of the earliest days of church history. Maybe you're familiar with this book, which describes the birth and explosive early growth of the church. If you are, I'd like to ask you to approach these next few pages with new eyes. Try to see the words you're about to read from a fresh perspective, as much as possible, as if you're seeing it and hearing it for the first time.

The setting: Peter, one of Jesus' closest friends and earliest followers, has just finished preaching in public, in the shadow of the temple in Jerusalem, just days after Jesus' ascension into heaven. He has urged his listeners—a crowd of thousands—to turn from their sins and turn to God, signifying their repentance by being baptized in the name of Jesus Christ.

Then, according to Acts 2:41–47:

> Those who accepted his message were baptized, and about three thousand were added to their number that day. They devoted themselves to the apostles' teaching and to the fellowship, to the breaking of bread and to prayer. Everyone was filled with awe, and many wonders and miraculous signs were done by the apostles. All the believers were together and had everything in common. Selling their possessions and goods, they gave to anyone as he had need. Every day they continued to meet together in the temple courts. They broke bread in their homes and ate together with glad and sincere hearts, praising God and enjoying the favor of all the people. And the Lord added to their number daily those who were being saved.[6]

Now, this passage is considered by scholars to be a snapshot of the early church, what it looked like and felt like and how it operated. And, to be fair, it sounds in some ways a *little* like what we do today. The description does reflect—*somewhat*, at least—how we operate as churches and Christ-followers in the twenty-first century.

But I want you to notice what is missing from that picture, and it's probably the main feature of what distinguishes "churchianity" today: *going to church*. At least as we use the phrase.

Of course, in those days there were no church buildings. (Steeples had not yet been invented, so how could there be?) So that may completely explain the glaring absence of that phrase, or anything like it.

But I don't think so. I think those 124 words we just read from the *New International Version* translation—116 words in the Greek—don't say *one word* about going to church on Sunday, Wednesday, or even Saturday night because those folks had a whole different vocabulary than we do, a whole different way of looking at things, and a whole different perspective.

Seeing the Church through New Eyes

Let's take a more thoughtful look at what it meant in those heady early days to be involved in this new thing Jesus had introduced, the "kingdom of God" he had ushered in.

First, "Those who accepted his message were baptized." Baptism was (and still is today) a ceremony that signified repentance and cleansing and being raised to new life. It was the immediate action people took to indicate that their lives had taken a turn, that they were making a drastic change, and that they would henceforth be following Jesus, who (by the way) was himself baptized. Interestingly, it doesn't say they came forward in a church service, or prayed a particular prayer, or anything like that. Those are all things we tend to associate with becoming a follower of Christ, yet this passage refers to none of them. It says, simply, they were baptized—an act which, as author Tim Stafford points out, "is the act of an individual identifying with a group. . . . For those of us who follow Jesus' steps in baptism, that group is God's people the church."[7] These folks who accepted Peter's message immediately and completely identified with the followers of Jesus.

Acts 2 also describes these early Christ-followers by saying, "They devoted themselves to the apostles' teaching." They became hungry, voracious students of God's Word, and they applied themselves whole-heartedly to learning from Peter, James, John, and the others how to follow Jesus and seek the kingdom of God.

Next, the text says, "They devoted themselves . . . to the fellow-ship." That is, they formed a community. They didn't go to church on Sundays and then forget those people existed the rest of the week. They *devoted* themselves to each other—those who were like them and those who weren't, those they liked and those they didn't like, those they got along with and those they couldn't stand. There were no "lone Christians" among them. No one was flying solo. They were devoted to each other.

The account continues: "They devoted themselves . . . to the break-ing of bread." This is a reference to their worship gatherings, where they met in homes to celebrate communion, a ceremony rich in symbolism in which they worshipped God by remembering and reflecting on Jesus' love for them as displayed in his sacrifice on the cross.

This is all terribly significant. You see, they did not "go to church" per se; this was not "putting in their time," "fulfilling their duty," or any such thing. This was about experiencing God, worshipping him, thank-ing him, and so on. They were *devoted* to experiencing God in worship.

The text also says, "They devoted themselves . . . to prayer." They were passionate about drawing closer to God, crying out to him, listening to him, telling him their needs, and pouring out their praise. Significantly (and unlike far too many of our churches today), prayer was apparently not something tucked away in a corner, something undertaken by a few ultra-dedicated prayer warriors. It seems the same folks who were devoted to fellowship and worship were also devoted to prayer.

The description of these proto-Christians in Acts 2 then says, "Everyone was filled with awe, and many wonders and miraculous signs were done by the apostles." People were being changed. They were not the same people they'd always been. They were noticeably different. They were being healed. They were growing. They weren't satisfied to be in each other's presence for an hour or so a week. No, man, this was too exciting. They were filled with awe!

Not only that, but "All the believers were together and had everything in common. Selling their possessions and goods, they gave to anyone as he had need." This verse reiterates the fact that they were a community. They weren't all the *same*, but they were all *together*. And they functioned as a community, giving and serving, back and forth.

The text says next, "Every day they continued to meet together in the temple courts. They broke bread in their homes and ate together with glad and sincere hearts, praising God and enjoying the favor of all the people." In other words, they didn't huddle inside a church building for an hour or two a week and expect people to come to them; they took all their praise and worship and celebration and fellowship out in public and shared it with the world around them. They went public. They were outward-focused. They knew their mission, and they set out to accomplish it.

And the passage ends in verse 47 much the same way it started: "And the Lord added to their number daily those who were being saved." I believe that's a depiction not only of what the early church was like way back when, but what God wants us to be like today, you, me, all of us. But we're not.

We're not.

I know, we all lead busy lives. There are jobs to do and mortgage payments to make and soccer games to take the kids to. There are meetings to attend and dentist appointments to remember. All kinds of stuff. The fact is, some of us are doing absolutely great if we even make it to church each week. Some weeks that represents a huge effort and a major sacrifice, with all we've got going on.

So I'm not saying it's easy to go to church once a week. I'm just saying, don't mistake that for Christianity. Don't kid yourself into thinking that is the way of Jesus.

Because it's not.

Quit Going to Church

If my relationship with God consists of "going to church," I need to quit that. I need to quit "going to church" and start following Jesus. I need to quit "going to church" and seek the kingdom of God. I need to quit going to church and devote myself to the Word of God, to living in community with God's people, to worshipping him wholeheartedly, to drawing close to him in prayer, and to going public, reaching out and sharing it all with the world around me.

In Jesus' name, I tell you, that is God's will for me and you.

That is what it means to follow Jesus.

So I urge you: quit *going* to church—and start *being* the church.

And Acts 2:41–47 is what *being* the church looks like. Or, at least, what it *looked* like—in the first century. And, though that was long ago and far away, much of it translates just fine into our lives and times. But even so, it might help to use another model, another way of describing what *being* the church looks like. Briefly put, it's what the Nicene Creed talks about.

The Nicene what?

The Nicene Creed is a statement of faith that was put together by church leaders way back in the fourth century. Some churches recite it weekly in the course of worship. Others do so every once in a while, and even my very nontraditional church has done so occasionally.

It's called the Nicene Creed because it was drafted and approved by a church council meeting in a town called Nicaea. So it's a good thing they weren't meeting in Rabbit Hash, Kentucky, or Goose Pimple Junction, Virginia (though it could be fun to recite the Goose Pimple Creed together).

But I mention all this because there's a lovely phrase in the Nicene Creed that I believe nicely parallels Acts 2. It is a phrase that also expresses some of what I mean when I say "be the church" instead of merely "go to church."[8]

The phrase is this: "We believe in one holy catholic and apostolic Church." That short statement identifies three components of what it means to *be* the church. It paints a portrait of the church in three colors, three components that are not sequential—like points on a line—but cyclical and encompassing—like the revolutions of a wheel.

Join the Band and Share Its Life

I plead with you, if your Christianity consists primarily of going to church, change your way of thinking and behaving, lose that focus, and concentrate instead on being part of the *holy*, *catholic*, and *apostolic* Church.

Holy

That word *holy* refers to the spirituality of the church. It is the part of being the church that Acts 2 describes when it says, "They devoted themselves to the apostles' teaching and . . . to the breaking of bread and to prayer."[9]

"Being the church" means being *devoted* to drawing closer to God, through reading and study of the Scriptures, worship, prayer, baptism, communion, fasting, giving, and so on. "Being the church" is a dynamic, not static, way of life. "Being the church" means always moving, constantly progressing, and continuously "being transformed into his likeness with ever-increasing glory, which comes from the Lord, who is the Spirit."[10] You and I are "being the church" when we are following so

23

closely on the heels of our rabbi, Jesus, that we are (to use the sage Yose ben Yoezer's phrase) covered in the dust of his feet.[11]

Catholic

The Nicene Creed reminds us also to be a holy, *catholic,* and apostolic Church. This doesn't mean the Roman Catholic Church. It means universal, global, all of us together. In other words, *catholic* refers to the community of the church. As author Tim Stafford puts it, judging from the biblical model, "When people began to follow Jesus, they joined a band of disciples. . . . [Therefore, s]uccess is not when people raise their hands and say they have prayed to accept Jesus. Success is when people join the band and begin to share its life."[12]

This is the part of "being the church" that Acts 2 describes when it says:

> Those who accepted his message were baptized . . . [and] devoted themselves . . . to the fellowship. . . . Everyone was filled with awe. . . . All the believers were together and had everything in common. Selling their possessions and goods, they gave to anyone as he had need. Every day they continued to meet together in the temple courts. They . . . ate together with glad and sincere hearts.[13]

"Being the church" means being unified, connected with one another, and interdependent on each other. It means a Lone Ranger Christian is not *being* the church Christ calls us to be, because our spirituality is not strictly an individual spirituality; it is also a communal spirituality.

We draw closer to God as a family, we read and study the Scriptures in community, we worship *together*, pray *together*, celebrate baptism and communion *together*. We fast and feast, give and receive *together* with glad and sincere hearts. We learn from each other, we meet in small groups, we accept accountability, and we let other people correct us and encourage us. We laugh together and cry together, share our homes and our lives, and jump neck-deep into each other's sweetness and yuckiness and in-betweenness.

When Christ calls you to follow him, he calls you to *be* the church, not *go* to church. He calls us all to be one holy, catholic, and apostolic church.

Apostolic

That last word, *apostolic,* has been understood and interpreted in several ways, one of which is *based on the teaching of the apostles.* And, of course, every biblical church is apostolic in that sense. It has also been understood to mean *characterized by gift-based leadership* (that is, that people with gifts in church leadership—whether those people are called "apostle" or not—are leading the church).

But, as Brian McLaren points out in his book *A New Kind of Christian,* whether our church is based on the teaching of the apostles or led by apostolic leadership, we certainly can't say we are a "holy, catholic, and apostolic" church if we don't share the identity of the apostles as people who were sent out into the world on a mission, people who represented Jesus in the world, people who like him were not there to be served, but to serve.[14]

To *be* the church in this sense means that "what we do in here"— in the place where the community gathers—must "fill the streets out there" (to use the words of a popular worship song).[15] It requires that we know—and act like we know—that the church does not exist for the sake of those of us on the inside but to be a blessing to those who are still on the outside.

In other words, *apostolic* refers to the mission of the church. It is the part of being the church that Acts 2 describes when it says, "About three thousand were added to their number that day . . . and many wonders and miraculous signs were done by the apostles. . . . They [enjoyed] the favor of all the people. And the Lord added to their number daily those who were being saved."[16]

That's what being the church looks like.

If your "Christian walk," as we sometimes call it, consists of "going to church," I plead with you, in Jesus' name: give it up. Devote yourself instead to the apostolic mission that Jesus gives to everyone who becomes his follower.

The "Sent Ones"

Brian McLaren says, "For Christ, his 'called ones' (which is what the Greek term for 'church' really means) were also to be his 'sent ones.' He trained those whom he called to follow him as apprentices so that they could be sent in his ongoing mission to teach his good news."[17]

I believe in one holy, catholic, and apostolic church, just like the early church described in Acts 2. More than that, I want to *be* that holy, catholic, and apostolic church; in fact, why should I settle for "going to church" when I can "be the church," as Christ calls me to be? And why should you settle for anything less than that?

In fact, if you look closely at that passage in Acts 2:41–47, you might see not a linear structure but a cyclical one. In other words, those verses do not depict a progression as much as they describe a revolution. I've charted it for you, beginning with the first phrase of Acts 2:41 at the nine o'clock position and proceeding clockwise.

Looking at it this way helps us to see that *being* the church means our spirituality is experienced in community . . .

and our community turns us outward to mission . . .

and our mission draws us closer to God . . .

and our spirituality draws us closer to each other . . .

and our community draws us closer to those around us, and on and on, and round and round she goes . . . and where she stops, only God knows.

~⧉ *Prayer*

Lord God, Adonai, please reveal to me the degree to which I have settled for "going to church," instead of "being the church." Come anew to my all-too-human heart and mind, and ignite in me a willingness—no, more than that, a desire, a passion—to "be the church," that "holy, catholic, and apostolic church" that is the Body of Christ.

Lord, I would be truly a part of your "holy" church, devoting myself to prayer, worship, and communion, drawing closer and closer to you and seeking out more and more ways of experiencing your goodness and grace.

I would be your "catholic" church by

> *living in community,*
> *learning from others,*
> *laughing and crying with them,*
> *growing with a small group,*
> *drawing close to others in the church,*
> *casting my lot in with them, for better or worse,*
> *and sharing my life with them.*

And I would be your "apostolic" church, too, Lord, by

> *reaching out,*
> *serving my church, my community, my world,*
> *going wherever you send me,*
> *sharing your love with those around me,*
> *and living out in my life the spirituality, community, and*

mission to which you call your whole church, to which I belong, together with all the saints in heaven and on earth.

In Jesus' name. Amen.

CHAPTER TWO

Quit Saying Your Prayers

Let's be honest. To most of us, prayer is a drag. It's drudgery. We have no interest in it, really. We may bow our heads at mealtime and mutter vague words of gratitude and blessing—which, by the way, is another thing we don't think about. What do we *mean* when we say "bless this food"? Didn't God already bless it when he sent the rain to grow the corn and the sun to get the fruit nice and ripe? Are we asking him to make the food tastier or more nutritious than the food our pagan neighbors are eating?

I think God has already blessed the food—in most cases, anyway—and in my case, he blesses it again through the expert work of my wife, the lovely Robin, who makes it taste amazing and keeps me roughly forty pounds overweight. But by the time I sit down to say grace, as we put it, God has already done his work; I think my contribution is to thank him and eat it, with gratitude, good manners, and possibly a little bit of moderation, if I can manage it.

That's exactly the sort of thing I'm talking about. Much of the time, those of us who do say grace over a meal give our words no more thought than when we taught our kids to pray, "If I should die before I wake."

And that prompts me to ask: What kind of creepy prayer is that to teach a kid? Especially as a bedtime prayer. It's basically saying, "Honey, I want you to go to sleep now, and just before I leave you all alone in a dark room, I want you to think about dying in your sleep, okay? Night night."

Maybe we really didn't think that one through, when we went and taught it to our kids, as if we were singing them a lullaby:

Lullaby and good night,
Go to sleep, though you might die . . .

When we *do* stop and think about it, we may come to see that this area—the prayers we say—is one in which we think and act in ways that bear only a slight resemblance (if they bear any resemblance at all) to the way of Jesus and the lives of the people of God as depicted in the Bible.

Even if we don't consider prayer a drag, we may approach it as a duty much of the time. We pray because we're supposed to. It's what we do. We say prayers at mealtimes and bedtime. We say prayers when we come to church and maybe when we start a meeting. And if we were to stop and think about it, if we were to ask ourselves, "Why are we doing this?", if we were honest, we would probably have to answer most often, "Because we're supposed to." It's a duty.

To be fair, of course, to some of us prayer is not so much a drag, or even a duty. But it *is* a discipline. It's one of those things we make ourselves do, because it's good for us. It's like eating right or exercising; we may not particularly enjoy it or look forward to it, and it's certainly not the *most* fun we have all day, but it's worthwhile because it builds our spiritual life and makes us more like Christ, and that's what we want. So we endure the discipline in order to enjoy the benefits.

But you know what? I've come to think that such ideas of prayer—such attitudes and approaches—have virtually nothing to do with the lives God wants us to lead, the faith he wants us to enjoy, and the kingdom of God Jesus came to usher in.

I think the ways we pray more often reflect "churchianity" than "Christianity."

Christianity vs. Churchianity

When Jesus came to earth, grew up as a Galilean Jew, and gathered around him a group of disciples, he modeled a way of praying that was either totally revolutionary or a revival of something long-forgotten.

How can I say that?

I can say it because the Bible records that Jesus' closest followers—twelve Jewish men who had learned to pray before they were knee-high to a menorah—nonetheless one day came to Jesus and said, "Lord, teach us to pray."[18]

Now, think about that.

These were Jews. Jewish *men*, who had prayed all their lives. They prayed every morning as soon as they awoke. They said a prayer as they dressed. They prayed before leaving the house. They prayed the *Birchot HaShachar*, the "eighteen blessings," every day of their lives, praising and thanking the God who made them Israelites, who made them in his image, who did not make them slaves, and who provided their needs. They prayed the *Shema* three times daily. They'd seen their parents pray. They'd seen priests pray. They'd seen rabbis and Pharisees and Sadducees pray.

But what Jesus did was apparently something else entirely. He had shown them something different, something new, something that didn't look at all like drudgery, duty, or even discipline to them. It was something that made them say, "We want that. Teach us to do that."

I believe at least part of what they saw was that Jesus did not just "say prayers," though he often used the same words as others did; he *kept company with God.* He communed with his Father, just like Peter and James and John communed with Jesus as they hiked from Galilee to Judea, or sat in a circle dipping pieces of bread into a big bowl of hummus, or laughed and danced together at a wedding feast.

These Jewish men saw their rabbi sharing life with the Father in much the same way they shared life with him. They saw him keeping company with Abba, and enjoying it, and being energized by it, in much the same way they wanted to hang around with Jesus, and ask him favors, and have him tease them, and not miss a word he said. And they wanted in on that.

Who wouldn't? I know I want the same thing. And I bet you do, too.

In Good Company

In fact, I believe that kind of praying is implicit in an oft-misunderstood verse of the Bible, one most churchgoers have heard many times. But we may never have heard it the way Jesus intends us to hear it. It's from the last book of the Bible. I believe these are the words of Jesus to me and you: "Here I am! I stand at the door and knock. If anyone hears my voice and opens the door, I will come in and eat with him, and he with me."[19]

Now, for years, "churchianity" has taken that verse and taught it and preached it and made it into a nice little verse about opening your heart to Jesus and becoming "born again." And I don't want to burst anyone's bubble, but I must tell you: that's not what the verse is about.

Revelation 3:20 is a portion of a letter which the risen Jesus dictated and which John his disciple relayed to a *church* in a town called Laodicea. It was not written to skeptics and seekers. It was not written to people attending an evangelistic service or responding to an altar call. It was written specifically to church folk who were being urged to repent and turn from their lukewarm ways.

And Jesus said, in effect, "Hey, open up. I want to come in. I want to eat with you. *I want to keep company with you.*"

Author Brennan Manning helps me appreciate this verse when he writes:

Sadly, the meaning of meal sharing is largely lost in the Christian community today. In the Near East, to share a meal with someone is a guarantee of peace, trust, fraternity, and forgiveness: the shared table symbolizes a shared life. For an orthodox Jew to say, "I would like to have dinner with you," is a metaphor implying "I would like to enter into friendship with you." Even today an American Jew will share a donut and a cup of coffee with you, but to extend a dinner invitation is to say: "Come to my *mikdash me-at*, the miniature sanctuary of my dining room table where we will celebrate the most sacred and beautiful experience that life affords—friendship."[20]

That is what Zacchaeus heard and understood when Jesus said, "Dude, come out of that tree. I want to come to your house. I want to eat with you. I would like to keep company with Zacchaeus the tax-collector."[21] The religious snots of the day got so upset with Jesus because he wasn't just accepting a social invitation; he was saying, "I want to *keep company* with tax-collectors, lepers, and prostitutes."

And Jesus wants to keep company with you, too. That's what prayer is. That's what it should be, anyway. That's what Jesus longs for, with you.

He doesn't frown on "God is great, God is good," but he won't be satisfied with that. He wants each of us to keep going, to move past "Bless us, O Lord, and these thy gifts" to the kind of conversation we enjoy when we lift our heads from prayer and turn to the person next to us and, smiling, say, "Hey, did you notice Sharla's hairdo in church today?" Believe it or not, he actually wants in on that stuff. He takes just as much delight (or dismay) in Sharla's hairdo as anyone does. And I wonder how many times we break his heart at the dinner table when we say "Amen" and then proceed to elbow him aside in order to enjoy true fellowship . . . with everyone but him.

Philip Yancey, in his book titled simply *Prayer*, writes:

I am writing away from home, sequestered in the mountains in the middle of winter. At the end of each day I talk with my wife, Janet, about the events of the day. I tell her how many words I wrote and what obstacles I met in the process, what Nordic ski or snowshoe trails I explored . . . which prepackaged frozen foods I ate for dinner. She tells me about the progress of her nagging cold, the mail that has been accumulating in my absence, the neighbors she has encountered walking their dogs to the mailboxes down the road. We discuss the weather, current events, news from relatives, upcoming social engagements. In essence, we meditate on the day with each other, in the process bringing the details into a new light.

Then, he says, "What I have just described bears a striking resemblance to prayer, too. Prayer, according to one ancient definition, is 'keeping company with God.'"[22]

I believe that is what God wants from each one of us. And *for* each one of us. He wants us to quit saying our prayers, if that's all we're doing, and instead *keep company with him.* Every day. Throughout the day. When we're alone and when we're with others.

Keeping Company with God

Now, what that looks like for you might be a little different from what it looks like for me. For you it might mean (as it did for author Henri Nouwen) rising from bed in the morning, pouring a cup of coffee, and sitting in a chair for fifteen minutes or so, starting with the words, "Good morning, Lord." You might tell him about your hopes and plans and fears and worries for the day, or you might ask him to tell you his. And maybe, at the end of the day, you might do like Philip Yancey did with his wife and just review the day, maybe tell him what's on your mind, and then maybe say, "Good night, Lord," before turning out the light.

Or you might do as monks and mystics have done for centuries and stop six or seven times in the course of a day to pray, briefly, starting with the psalmist's phrase, "O God, come to my assistance; O Lord, make haste to help me." If you prefer simpler words, you could start out with words like, "Here I am, Lord." The important thing is not so much the words you use as the habit you pursue; in fact, one great value of short and regular times of prayer throughout each day is that they make it much easier to "chat" with God, as one does with any friend. You'll be far more likely to reach a point of real authenticity in such frequent conversations (even if they're brief), haggling with God (like Abraham[23]), complaining to him (like the psalmists[24]), asking his advice (like David[25]), and wrestling with him (like Jacob[26]). And you might also find that doing so tends to encourage an awareness of God's presence that pretty much lasts all day long, transforming the times in between your times of prayer . . . into times of prayer.

This was my experience on my first weeklong prayer retreat at the Abbey of Gethsemani, a famous monastery near Louisville, Kentucky. I am not rhapsodizing to say that week changed my life. I arrived on a Friday, checked into a simple guest room, and decided to join the monks—at least for the first twenty-four hours I was there—in their observance of the Opus Dei (work of God) that constitutes the rhythm of the monks' lives. They meet for prayer seven times a day:

> *vigils* (3:15 A.M.)
>
> *lauds* (5:45 A.M.)
>
> *terce* (7:30 A.M.)
>
> *sext* (12:15 P.M.)
>
> *none* (2:15 P.M.)
>
> *vespers* (5:30 P.M.)
>
> *compline* (7:30 P.M.)

Seven times a day. Every day. I had arrived just in time for lunch on the first day—which meant that my first prayer time was *none*—so, after *none*, *vespers*, *compline*, *vigils*, *lauds*, *terce*, and *sext*, I went immediately, like all the others, monks and non-monks alike, to lunch. I silently descended the staircase from the sanctuary to the dining room, silently filed through the cafeteria line, silently filled my tray with food, silently walked to an empty chair, and silently sat down. That's when it happened. I bowed my head over my tray to say grace . . . and realized I was already praying. There was no need to start praying because, just one full day into the rhythm of that community, I found myself no longer "starting" and "finishing" my times of prayer; I did not "enter" and "exit" God's presence. I had been praying since I began my day. Since that retreat, I have cultivated and guarded an experience I had previously thought was a practical impossibility: that of praying "without ceasing"[27] throughout the day.

Anthony Bloom, the head of the Russian Orthodox church in Western Europe from 1963-1974, developed a similar habit in the midst of a demanding administrative and ecclesiastical schedule. He developed the habit of stopping his workday at set times and saying out loud, "I am seated, I am doing nothing, I will do nothing for five minutes. . . . I am here in the presence of God, in my own presence and in the presence of all the furniture that is around me, just still, moving nowhere." At first, he did this for just a few minutes each time, but eventually he developed the ability to consciously keep company with God throughout the day, as these "rest stops" combined with his morning and evening prayers to create an all-day awareness of God's presence.[28]

Or you might do the sort of thing orthodox Jews do every year when they celebrate Passover and leave an extra chair and place setting at the table, as a way of inviting and anticipating the coming of Elijah who the Bible said would precede the coming of Messiah. You might leave an empty chair at the table or next to your bed, perhaps, that will help you keep company with Jesus, as you imagine him sitting next to you, sharing in your life and conversation as he longs to do.

A Place to Put Your Head

In his book *Abba's Child*, Brennan Manning tells the story of an old man who was dying of cancer, and the man's daughter asked the local priest to come and pray with her father. When the priest arrived, he found the man lying in bed with his head propped up on two pillows, and there was an empty chair beside his bed.

"I guess you were expecting me," the priest said.

"No," the man answered. "Who are you?"

"I'm the new associate at your church," the priest replied. "When I saw the empty chair, I figured you knew I was going to show up."

"Oh yeah, the chair," said the bedridden man. "Would you mind closing the door?"

So he shut the door.

"I've never told anyone this, not even my daughter," said the man, "but all my life I have never known how to pray. I used to hear the pastor talk about prayer, but it always went right over my head. Finally I said to him one day in sheer frustration, 'I get nothing out of your sermons on prayer.'

"'Here,' says my pastor, reaching into the bottom drawer of his desk. 'Read this book by Hans Urs von Balthasar. He's a Swiss theologian. It's the best book on contemplative prayer in the twentieth century.'

"Well," said the man, "I took the book home and tried to read it. But in the first three pages I had to look up twelve words in the dictionary. I gave the book back to my pastor, thanked him, and under my breath whispered, 'for nothin'.'"

"I abandoned any attempt at prayer," he continued, "until one day about four years ago, my best friend said to me, 'Joe, prayer is just a simple matter of having a conversation with Jesus. Here's what I suggest. Sit down on a chair, place an empty chair in front of you, and in faith see Jesus on the chair. It's not spooky, because He promised, "I'll be with you all days." Then just speak to Him, and listen in the same way you're doing with me right now.'

"So I tried it, and I've liked it so much that I do it a couple of hours every day. I'm careful, though. If my daughter saw me talking to an empty chair, she'd either have a nervous breakdown or send me off to the funny farm."

The priest was deeply moved by the story and encouraged the old guy to continue on his prayer journey. Then he prayed with him and returned to the church. Two nights later, the daughter called to tell the priest that her daddy had died that afternoon.

"Did he seem to die in peace?" he asked.

"Yes," she said. "When I left the house around 2:00, he called me over to his bedside, told me one of his corny jokes, and kissed me on the cheek. When I got back from the store an hour later, I found him dead."

And then she paused, as if she weren't sure she should go on. But she did, and she said, "But there was something strange—in fact, beyond strange, kind of weird. . . . It has to do with how I found him."

"How you found him?" the priest asked.

She nodded. "Apparently," she said, "just before Daddy died, he leaned over and rested his head on a chair beside his bed."[29]

Jesus longs for such intimacy with you. He wants to keep company with you. He says, "Here I am! I stand at the door and knock. If anyone hears my voice and opens the door, I will come in and eat with him, and he with me."[30]

He says, "Come to my *mikdash me-at*, the dinner table where we will celebrate the most sacred and beautiful experience that life affords—my friendship with you, and your friendship with me."

He invites you.

He aches for you.

He longs for your company.

So quit saying prayers . . . and focus your efforts, your enthusiasm, your hopes, and your dreams on keeping company with God.

~☙ *Prayer*

Lord Jesus, thank you for your insistent knock at the door of my heart . . . the door of my life.

Show me how to keep company with you. Teach me how to include you in the rhythms and responsibilities of my day. Help me, like Zacchaeus, to jump at the chance to eat with you, and spend time with you. Enable me to share my life with you, to learn to chat with you, to tell you what I'm thinking, to listen as you tell me what you're thinking, and even haggle, complain, consult, and wrestle with you as I go through my day.

I open to you. I will save a chair for you. Come in, Lord. Amen.

CHAPTER THREE

Quit Reading Your Bible

You can learn a lot by reading.

I was reading the *Weekly World News* not too long ago. I don't know if you've heard of this popular newspaper, but it started publishing in 1979, and in the mid-1980s reached a circulation of 1.3 million, touting itself as "The World's Only Reliable Newspaper." Keep that in mind.

In just one issue, I read a ton of things I never knew before—and would never have known if I had confined my reading to, say, the *New York Times* or the *Wall Street Journal*. I learned about an alien training camp near the South Pole, in which "ETs Sharpen Invasion Skills in Mock Town." I learned about a college in Kentucky that was selling burial plots in their football stadium end zone. And I learned that Bigfoot has been making pottery in the Okefenokee swamp . . . a discovery supported by photographic proof!

That's amazing, I know. But I'm not finished. Not nearly. Reading *Weekly World News* also enlarged my Bible knowledge.

No kidding!

On page eleven of that very issue, I discovered that an archaeological excavation in the Sinai Peninsula uncovered two ancient tablets that Moses left behind on Mount Sinai, containing an addendum to the Ten Commandments, "ten additional 'suggestions' on how to lead a good life." These suggestions reportedly included, "Thou shalt not adhere to seats the gum of thy chewing," and "Thou shalt admit not latecomers to thy place in line."[31]

I kid you not. The article even quoted an expert: an enthusiastic Dr. Benjamin Levi of the Cairo Biblical Center. So it must be true.

But that's not all. The hits just kept coming. Amazingly, in the very same issue, was a report of an American tourist on vacation in the Egyptian desert who encountered a burning bush. And the bush not only told the guy—"forty-year-old Detroit native Dave Berger"—that it was the same bush that had spoken to Moses, but that—brace yourself—unless people started to follow the commandments (all *twenty* of them, the bush said, "as reported in *Weekly World News*"), God would soon destroy the world and start building humankind from scratch.

Best of all, when Mr. Berger asked why God chose to speak to him through the burning bush, "It replied that this was by no means a well-traveled path and there was no one else to address."[32]

Pretty convincing stuff. Stuff that kinda makes you go, "Hmm." But, as amazing as it is, it's still not the Bible. It's nothing like the Bible. But probably not for the reasons you might think.

Why We Read

Anyone will tell you that if you want to follow Christ, Bible reading is a big part of it, right? You're supposed to pray, read your Bible, and go to church. Those are so fundamental, you could call them Christianity 101. But the Bible is not the *Weekly World News*. You probably already knew that. For too long, however, too many of us have tended to act as though it is. We read it for at least some of the same reasons people might read *Weekly World News*—or the *Weekly Reader*, for that matter—and with pretty much the same results. How we treat and how we approach the Bible are among the ways in which I believe we've departed from the way of Jesus and the kind of lives God intends for us to enjoy.

Think about it: Why do people read anything? I can suggest at least five reasons.

Entertainment

Perhaps the most widespread reason people read is for the entertainment value it affords. That has to be why *Weekly World News* exists, right? I mean, it has jokes, puzzles, comics, pictures, and more. That's entertainment!

This is the main reason folks read *People* or *Mad* magazine. It's why people read about Harry Potter or Winnie the Pooh. It's why Dave Barry's or Tina Fey's books are bestsellers.

My wife even finds a strange kind of enjoyment in reading billboards and street signs. Out loud. To me. While we're riding together in the car. I haven't yet discerned any particular pattern to which signs she finds interesting and which she doesn't. She is just as likely to read from a billboard that says, "Advertise Here," as she is likely to repeat the words "Lois Lane" from a street sign, before asking, "Why does that sound familiar?"

But she does it because it helps pass the time and entertains her (and sometimes—but not always—others in the car).

Escape

Reading for escape is related to reading for entertainment, but it goes much deeper. Some people read in order to forget their worries, get away from their lives, and get lost in a book.

Some people became voracious readers in the first place because of unhappy childhoods, unfulfilled dreams, or stressful jobs. It helps to check out *Weekly World News* and read the amazing predictions of Chuck Lee, who "discovered that eating large amounts of hot mustard enabled him to foretell the future," including his prediction that in the year 2023, people will be eating so many vegetables that their blood will turn green, creating a new condition called high "chloresterol."[33] I kid you not.

Not everyone finds their escape in the *Weekly World News,* however. Others love to get swept up and carried away by a glittery travel magazine, an eight-hundred-page fantasy novel, or a paperback romance.

Information

People also read for information. A good percentage of a student's reading material falls in this category, whether he or she is studying for a history exam or preparing for a science fair demonstration. And most of us continue long after school lets out for the summer—or the decade—to read for information.

You read the restaurant menu to find a dining choice that satisfies your hunger without emptying your bank account. You peruse the newspaper to learn about what's going on the world around you. You study the issues to prepare for the next election. You scan the classifieds for a better job or a good used car.

Instruction

We also read for instruction. "How to Win the Lottery." "No-Diet Weight Loss." "Eight Braided Styles to Wear Now." "Get Rid of Stress." "Quilt Your Way to Mental Health." (I may have made up that last one.)

We seek out instruction in many different forms. School textbooks, sure. But also cooking magazines. How-to books. Auto repair manuals. Installation instructions.

You may be in a field of work that requires regular reading for instruction: to keep current on investment trends, for example. Or to learn about new heart surgery techniques. Or to stay abreast of new laws and regulations that affect your industry.

Inspiration

And, of course, we also read for inspiration. This is why Max Lucado is such a successful writer. It's why people read Tony Robbins. Or the billion different versions of *Chicken Soup for the Soul*. (I think the only one they haven't yet released is *Chicken Soup for the Chicken's Soul*, but I wouldn't be surprised to see it real soon.)

Depending on your personality and preferences, you may read poetry to get inspired. Or biographies. Or great literature. Or real-life accounts of people who overcame impossible circumstances on their way to unforeseen success. Or your reading may inspire you to learn that others have faced the same challenges you have and yet triumphed.

The Book of Books

You probably know it already, but the Bible can be all of those things. Parts of it are entertaining, even funny (such as Jesus' stand-up routine about the friend at midnight in Luke 11, which is a comedic masterpiece if understood in its cultural context). It can provide an escape for someone who wants to get lost in a good story (such as the book of Jonah) or swept up in a beautiful poem (such as the Song of Songs). Much of it is chock-full of information as well as instruction and certainly inspiration. But if that's what you're getting out of reading your Bible, I want to urge you to quit.

That's right. You heard me: Quit reading your Bible.

The Bible wasn't given to you primarily for those reasons. And the fact is, I think most of us end up perverting or controverting its real purpose, its true function, because we read the Bible in such a way as to miss the point . . . and maybe even break God's heart.

How can I say such a thing? Let me try to explain. Step back with me, rewind *way* back to a time before there was a Bible, before Peter or Paul, before Isaiah or Daniel, before David or Solomon or Samuel, to part of a dialogue that took place between Moses and God himself.

Moses was the guy God spoke to in the burning bush—long before Dave from Detroit was born or the *Weekly World News* began publishing. In Exodus 33, the Bible records a conversation that took place after Moses had gone back into Egypt, faced down the mighty Pharaoh, announced the ten plagues, led the whole Jewish population out of slavery in Egypt, parted the Red Sea, received the Ten Commandments on Mount Sinai, and then shattered them when he came down from the mountain and saw that his people had already turned to idolatry. Then he went back into the presence of God.

And Exodus 33:11 says, "The LORD would speak to Moses face to face, as a man speaks with his friend."

If we could somehow shed our personal spiritual experiences, along with two thousand years of church history and a few thousand more of Israel's history, and get back to the moment that short verse describes, we would be shocked to read those sixteen words. The idea of God speaking to a human being face-to-face, as a man speaks to a friend, would be nearly impossible to wrap our minds around. It might induce a migraine headache. It would astound and amaze us . . . as it should do even today.

But it is perhaps what Moses said to God that ought to interest us even more. Because it may just reveal how incomplete and inadequate are our usual reasons for reading the Bible. Take a moment to read—slowly—what Moses said to God, as it is recorded in the Bible:

> Moses said to the LORD, "You have been telling me, 'Lead these people,' but you have not let me know whom you will send with me. You have said, 'I know you by name and you have found favor with me.' If you are pleased with me, teach me your ways so I may know you and continue to find favor with you. Remember that this nation is your people."[34]

Do you see what Moses said? He said, "Teach me your ways." Why?

So I can be entertained?

So I can escape from my problems?

So I can get information? Instruction? Inspiration?

No. He said, "Teach me your ways so I may know you."

I think that is huge. I think it is unspeakably important, immeasurably profound. And it ought to be almost unbearably convicting.

You see, the Bible is the Word of God. It is a compendium of his ways. It is often entertaining. It is definitely informative and instructive. It is the most inspirational book ever written. But that Word, those stories and letters, those poems and proverbs, those historical accounts and glittering visions are given to us *as if* in answer to Moses' request: God has shown us his ways *so we might know him,* so we can relate to him, so we can receive his love and love him back.

The Bible is not primarily information or instruction or inspiration. It is given to us as an instrument of relationship.

RSVP

Think back—painful though it may be—to those awkward, terrifying seventh- or eighth-grade romances of your youth. I hope you can do so without any traumatic episodes. I can't, but I hope you can.

Imagine if you had written a hopeful love note to the person of your dreams:

Do you like me?
❑ Yes ❑ No ❑ Maybe
Check one.

If that memory is too painful, fast forward past eighth grade and think about writing a love letter a few years later, a letter in which you opened your heart and proclaimed your love and told everything that was in your heart for that special other person on whom all your hopes and dreams had settled.

What sort of response would you hope for?

Would it be something that said, "I was so happy to receive your letter. It sure did break up my boredom. It was so entertaining. I hope you'll write more."

Chances are, that wouldn't be what you'd want to hear, would it? A response such as that would have been a bitter disappointment, wouldn't it?

How about a response like, "I got your letter just in time. It helped me forget my troubles. I was able to escape for a few moments from my real life."

That wouldn't quite do it, either, would it?

What about a response like this one: "Your letter was wonderful. I learned so much about proper grammar and good handwriting."

That still wouldn't do the trick, would it?

Maybe: "Your letter is a great model for me. The next time I write a love letter, I'm going to use it as a framework."

Or: "I must tell you, your letter touched my heart and made me believe in myself and gave me hope for the future."

There's something to be said for each of those responses, but none of them would be what your heart hoped for, right? None of them would fulfill the purpose of your love letter. Wouldn't you, if you wrote a love letter, hope to hear back something like, "I love you, too. I love you for writing the things you wrote. I love you for confessing your love to me. I love you for taking the time to write. I love you for just being you. I love you. I can't tell you enough. I love you."

Do you see the difference?

Do you think your God, your Abba, your Heavenly Father, is so different?

Do you think he is less of a lover than you?

Do you think he has superintended the writing, collection, compilation, and preservation of his Word for your *entertainment?* For your *information*? Or even for your *inspiration*?

Don't you think he wants you, like Moses, to know his *ways* so you might know *him*? Can't you imagine that he wrote so many words over so many years through so many people to facilitate a love relationship with you?

If so, then please quit reading your Bible the way you read a newspaper or a magazine or a book. Quit reading your Bible as you read a parking ticket or credit card bill. Eugene Peterson suggests we bring "the leisure and attentiveness of lovers to this text," adding, "Lovers don't take a quick look, get a 'message' or a 'meaning,' and then run off and talk endlessly with their friends about how they feel."[35] Approach your Bible as a lover: combing over it, cherishing it, responding to it, delighting in it. Learn to enjoy the Bible as the means by which you relate to the God who in its pages opens his heart and proclaims his love and tells you everything that is in his heart for you.

Relational Reading

At this point, you may be saying, "Uh, okay, Bob. Sounds good. But how do I do that?"

Well, look at what Moses did. After he said, "Teach me your ways so I may know you," the Bible says, "The LORD replied, 'My Presence will go with you, and I will give you rest.'"[36]

What did Moses do there? Well, he *listened*, right? He spoke, then God spoke, and Moses listened.

Few of us *ever* do that.

We read God's words . . . but we never listen. We just go on to the next line, and then the line after that, without pausing to make sure we hear what God is saying.

My wife, the lovely Robin, and I were on a mission trip to Mexico a few years ago, and several times we ate a peanut butter and jelly sandwich lunch on the bus en route from one place to another. Our host remarked that the locals would laugh at us if they could see us eating that way, because they think Americans' habit of eating "on the run," of grabbing carryout or a quick bite, is so strange.

That sort of eating, they would say, misses the point. From their perspective, the experience of having a meal isn't about getting calories in our bellies; it is a communal experience, something we share with others around the table or the campfire. To eat alone, to "grab a bite," is leaving out the best part of the process. It's like throwing out the baby while keeping the bathwater.

It's that way for most of us in our reading of God's Word . . . if we find time to read it at all. We read on the run. We read to get it done. We read to keep up with our read-the-Bible-in-a-year plan.

But that short-circuits the reason God gave us his Word in the first place. It cheats us of the true blessing in store for us. It robs us of the experience the prophet Jeremiah talked about when he said, "When your words came, I devoured them: your word was my delight and the joy of my heart."[37]

Many centuries ago, some followers of Jesus developed an exercise called *lectio divina*, which means, literally, "divine reading." It is a different way of reading, one that fosters relationship rather than merely providing entertainment or absorbing information. It involves learning to read in a new way, slowly and prayerfully, devouring every word and allowing it to seep deep down. It means spending time not just with the words, not just with the text, but with the Lord of the text, reading and rereading, as you would read good poetry, as you would sip a cup of tea, letting its warmth on a cold winter day roll over your tongue and flow down your throat until it fills you slowly and all over with its sweetness and warmth.

While there is no one correct way to practice this ancient method, it is usually broken down into four distinct stages. Each one is typically identified by a Latin word: lectio, meditatio, oratio, and contemplatio. Please consider trying it, if you're interested in approaching the Bible as a means of relationship with God. You might begin a reading period with a short time of silence and a simple prayer asking God to draw you into his presence as you read.

Lectio

Select a passage or verse—or even a single sentence or word. (Remember, the purpose is not to "get through" a passage or accomplish a goal, but to spend time with God and get to know and love him better.) Read the text slowly and reflectively. Don't try to understand, but concentrate instead on absorbing the words and letting them settle into your mind and heart. You may read the text more than once, perhaps slowing down with each reading. Or you might first read the text silently, then *listen* to someone read it aloud (or to a recording), then follow along in the text while listening, then read it aloud yourself. I find it helpful to hear a verse or passage read by different voices, preferably male and female.

Meditatio

The next part of the process involves listening. Try to listen prayerfully, aware of God's presence and attentive to his voice. Try not to merely hear the words, but hear his voice in the words. Try to listen not only with your ears, but also with your mind, heart, and spirit for what God might be saying. Roll over the words of the text in your mind. Listen for the "still, small voice" of God in what you've just read. If a phrase or word from the reading seems to impress itself on you, hold it in your mind. Repeat it to yourself. Think about it. Consider how God is reaching out to you through that phrase or word.

Oratio

In oratio, the reader speaks to God—internally or externally—as Moses did, "face to face, as a man speaks with his friend." Speak naturally, conversationally. Tell God whatever enters your mind. Ask questions. Respond to whatever you think he is saying to you, whether that involves confession and repentance, surrender and submission, praise and thanks, or petition. Through it all, focus on the pleasure of his presence and how he might want to use the text to draw you closer and make himself known to you.

Contemplatio

In the final moments of lectio divina, focus on simply resting in God's embrace, basking in his love for you, and enjoying his closeness. You may want to do so in silence, or you may decide to repeat a phrase or word several times, such as, "I love you," or "You are here." I often enter this final part of lectio with the old Nestea television commercial in mind—the one where someone is holding a glass of tea in his hand while freefalling backward into a swimming pool. That is, I visualize myself letting go and taking a "Nestea Plunge" into God's arms, abandoning myself to him, relaxing and reposing in his presence. Then, when my time of lectio divina concludes, my aim is always to continue in God's presence, whatever I may turn my mind or hand to next.

Lectio divina is not the only way to read the Bible as an aid to relationship with God. But for many people, it provides a breakthrough experience that turns Bible reading in a new direction.

Trust God with What's Already Inside You

Over the years, lectio divina has changed my Bible reading into a communal experience, like a pleasant meal shared with a friend—and that has immeasurably affected my relationship with God. But there's something else I noticed in Moses's exchange with the Lord in Exodus 33. Look at verses 15–16: "Then Moses said to him, 'If your Presence does not go with us, do not send us up from here. How will anyone know that you are pleased with me and with your people unless you go with us? What else will distinguish me and your people from all the other people on the face of the earth?'"

Do you see what's happening there? Moses is answering God. He is pleading with God. More than that, he's actually arguing with God. He's relating to God . . . as if . . . God is a . . . *real* person.

Shocking, right?

But it shouldn't be shocking at all. God *is* a real person, and he wants a real relationship with you, not a relationship where you say only what is expected and never tell him what you're really feeling or thinking. He knows your inner thoughts and feelings anyway, so why not trust God with what's already inside you? Why not relate to him authentically? Honestly? Even vulnerably.

You know what that might look like? Let me see if I can show you what it sometimes looks like for me.

I might actually start out my reading with Moses's prayer, and whether I'm going to read a few chapters or just a verse or two, whether I'm going to read a psalm or one of those long genealogies, I might start out by praying, "Lord, teach me your ways so I may know you."

Then I might read a passage like this one in Exodus 33, where Moses said to God, "If your Presence does not go with us, do not send us up from here."[38]

And I might stop there, and say, "Lord, I want your presence more than anything. I want to spend time with you. I want to know that I've been in your presence. I want other people to know, when I leave here, that I've been in your presence. I want to carry the fragrance of your presence with me throughout this day, so please come to me now in such a way that our conversation will not end when I leave this place, but that every step I take will be taken in communion with you."

Or I might just as likely read that passage where Moses says to God, "If your Presence does not go with us, do not send us up from here," and I might pause to say, "Lord, you know I haven't felt your presence for some time now. What's that about? Where have you been? It's not like I haven't been faithful. It's not like I haven't plopped myself down in this prayer chair day after day. And yet still I'm exhausted. I feel empty—and you seem absent. So if you're going to keep this up, then please tell me."

In the next breath, I might stop for a moment, and say, "Yes, Lord, I do believe you are present even when I don't feel you. I know that—in my head—and I know you want me to be faithful even when I don't feel your presence. But I have enough faith to believe my presence brings you joy, because your Word says so. It says you delight in me . . . so can you help me feel some of that—in my heart? Can you please give me a sense of your pleasure?"

Then I might stop reading, or I might go on in this chapter, to the next couple of verses, and read: "And the LORD said to Moses, 'I will do the very thing you have asked, because I am pleased with you and I know you by name.' Then Moses said, 'Now show me your glory.'"[39]

And I might say, "Oh, Lord, if you would do that . . . if you would show me your glory, I would be so grateful. That's what I need, Lord. Show me your glory. Show me your presence. Show me your hand on my life. Show me I'm loved."

That was another thing Moses did in his Exodus 33 conversation with God; he actually claimed God's words for himself. He latched onto what God said he would do and said, "Now do it!" He had the audacity to say, "God, you said you would, so I'm asking you—do it, please!"

Of course, not every promise in the Bible pertains to me personally, but when I come across a verse that says, "The Lord . . . does not want anyone to be destroyed, but wants everyone to repent," I call him on that, and I pray for the people around me who don't yet know God's love, saying, "Lord, you say you don't want anyone to miss out on your kingdom, on eternal life . . . so please bring this person to repentance."[40]

When I read, "Blessed are those who mourn, for they will be comforted," I might say, "Lord, you say those who mourn should be happy, because of the comfort they will receive . . . so please send comfort to them."[41]

So when I read Moses saying, "Now show me your glory," I'm seeing a model of how—by God's grace—I can converse with God, and draw close to him and relate to him through his Word instead of just reading it.[42]

Then again, I might keep reading, since I'm almost to the end of the chapter, where God answers Moses's prayer, and it says: "Then the LORD said, 'There is a place near me where you may stand on a rock. When my glory passes by, I will put you in a cleft in the rock and cover you with my hand until I have passed by. Then I will remove my hand and you will see my back; but my face must not be seen.'"[43]

And that might just prompt me to bow in God's presence, and sing:

He hideth my soul in the cleft of the rock
That shadows a dry, thirsty land;
He hideth my life in the depths of His love,
And covers me there with His hand,
And covers me there with His hand.[44]

I believe God longs for something like that from us all. Not that he expects or desires you to relate to him and talk to him in the same ways I do, but I truly believe he wants us all to quit reading the Bible for entertainment or escape, or for information or instruction or inspiration alone, and instead start to hear his voice in his love letter to us. I think he longs for us to respond by saying, "I love you, too. I love you for writing the things you wrote. I love you for confessing your love to me. I love you for taking the time to write. I love you for just being you. I love you. I can't tell you enough. I love you."

So quit reading your Bible . . . and approach it and use it instead as a means to relationship with God.

~~§ *Prayer*

Abba, Father, thank you for your Word. Forgive me for the ways I've neglected it and misused it. Forgive me for responding so flippantly and inappropriately to your words of love.

Help me to see your love on every page. Help me to hear your voice in every line and every word. Help me not merely to read, but to devour every word and allow it to seep deep down. Teach me to spend time not just with the words, not just with the text, but with you, the Lord of the text, reading and reread-ing, listening and speaking, absorbing and enjoying, as I would sip a cup of tea, letting its warmth on a cold winter day roll over my tongue and flow down my throat until it fills me slowly and all over with its sweetness and warmth.

Teach me a new way of approaching and reading and experiencing your Word. Teach me your ways, that I may know you. Amen.

CHAPTER FOUR

Quit Sharing Your Faith

As I mentioned in an earlier chapter, I grew up going to church. I can't remember a time in my life when I didn't know God's love. I came to faith at an early age, in a children's church service, and grew in faith as I grew in size. I was also raised in a loving church with a history of servanthood and evangelism.

I vividly recall marching with the other kids in my children's church to a corner in the Over-the-Rhine section of Cincinnati, Ohio—which even way back then was an eye-opening part of the community—where we sang songs, told stories, and shared our love for God with anyone who would listen.

I've passed out tracts to people on boardwalks and at fairs. I've preached sermons and played Christian hymns on the mean streets of Manhattan. I've traipsed door-to-door, distributing Christian magazines. I've told my faith story to shoppers in upscale malls and to inmates of maximum security prisons. I've talked about God to men and women in bars and juke joints and go-go clubs. I've even been offered real cash money to go away . . . and I've taken it at least once.

In the course of all that, I've learned a handful of things. I've especially learned *what not to do*. For example, I can readily list ten ways *not* to start a spiritual conversation with someone.

Top Ten *Worst* Ways

Here are my top ten ways *not* to start a spiritual conversation.

10. Hey, baby! You sure are hot! But hell is even hotter . . .
9. What's your sign? Mine's the sign of the fish.
8. While we're waiting for the police to arrive, have you ever heard of the Four Spiritual Laws?
7. If you think it's hot here, try burning in the fires of hell.
6. What a cute puppy—er, baby you have there!
5. I bet you're wondering why each of my fingers is a different color.
4. You can't get to heaven on a Harley, you know.
3. Would you like fries with that . . . and, by the way, if you died tonight, do you know where you'd spend eternity?
2. This may be the liquor talking, but I think you need Jesus.

And the number one worst way to start a spiritual conversation with someone:

1. You look like a sinner—can we talk?

Now, I'm not saying those tactics would never work; I'm just saying I don't recommend them. In fact, in the interest of full disclosure, I really,

really didn't want to do most of those evangelistic efforts I described to you in the first few paragraphs of this chapter. Though, to be truthful, some of those efforts—maybe all of them, for all I know—actually met with success once in a while.

But while there are hundreds, thousands, even millions of ways for people to hear and respond to the good news about God's love and grace as revealed through Jesus Christ, I have come to suspect that the vast majority of us in the Western world, certainly in America, have missed the boat and misunderstood—even distorted—the way God intends for us to spread the influence of his kingdom and introduce more and more people to the love of God that is in Christ Jesus our Lord.

The Way We Are

Think of those "evangelistic" activities I described to you at the beginning of this chapter, things I've done in my young and exciting life, ways I've—often reluctantly—shared my faith, so to speak, with others. Take a few moments to ponder how each of them happens.

When I and the other kids in my children's church finished our little program in Over-the-Rhine, we marched back to the church building, and as far as I know, we never saw those folks again (at least not until our next "children's open-air meeting").

The people to whom I distributed tracts and free magazines and to whom I preached sermons and told my testimony—they were all complete strangers to me.

The prisoners and shoppers and juke joint customers—if I ever heard their names, I forgot them soon afterward.

Maybe it's just me—and it wouldn't be the first time I'm all alone in my musings—but if I take a sincere, open-minded look at the way of Jesus and the life of the early church, I don't see a lot of "sharing my faith" the way I "shared my faith" in the first forty-some years of my life. (And thank you for thinking I don't seem that old. That *is* what you were thinking, right?)

I think we've pretty completely and successfully *eviscerated* the good news of Jesus Christ by the way we *think about* and *do* evangelism.

Think about it: when the Father sent Jesus to this earth, he sent "the Word" to be conceived in a human womb, to be born into a human family, and to grow up in a human community. The Bible says, "The Word became flesh and made his dwelling among us."[45]

The Message paraphrases it like this: "The Word became flesh and blood, and moved into the neighborhood."[46]

When the time was right, the Father sent Jesus—the logos, the eternal, the pre-existent Word—to take up residence in human flesh and become:

Mary's son,
James's brother,
John's cousin,
Andrew's neighbor,
Philip's rabbi, and
Lazarus's best friend.

Call me crazy, but I think maybe we're supposed to learn something from that.

If the Father had sent the Word like we have traditionally spread the word, he would have sent Jesus to earth for a weekend, had him preach a few sermons or hand out a few tracts, and then brought him back to heaven. But that's not how he did it.

He put the Word into flesh. He incarnated the good news. The eternal God transformed himself into a regular guy, a neighbor, the kid down the street, a carpenter, a stonecutter, a country boy.

I'm not saying our way hasn't worked at all. God, in his matchless creativity, works his will in some of the most surprising people in some of the most startling ways. But I am saying that Jesus' way is certain to be the best way.

My friend Mike Erre, lead pastor of Mariners Church Mission Viejo in California, wrote the following in his book, *The Jesus of Suburbia*: "It is often suggested that evangelism is something we 'do' when we 'share' our faith with someone outside the Christian community.... [But that] traditional understanding of evangelism ... [is] too narrowly construed. The Bible teaches that *evangelism is life*."[47]

In other words, quit sharing your faith ... and share your *life*.

More Than Words

Consider the difference between the way we have typically approached sharing our faith and the Apostle Paul's method. He wrote to the new Christ-followers in a city called Thessalonica:

> It is clear to us, friends, that God not only loves you very much but also has put his hand on you for something special. When the Message we preached came to you, it wasn't just words.... You paid careful attention to the way we lived among you, and determined to live that way yourselves. In imitating us, you imitated the Master. Although great trouble accompanied the Word, you were able to take great joy from the Holy Spirit!— taking the trouble with the joy, the joy with the trouble.

Do you know that all over the provinces of both Macedonia and Achaia believers look up to you? The word has gotten around. Your lives are echoing the Master's Word, not only in the provinces but all over the place. The news of your faith in God is out. We don't even have to say anything anymore— you're the message!

. . . We never used words to butter you up. No one knows that better than you. And God knows we never used words as a smoke screen to take advantage of you. We were never patronizing, never condescending, but we cared for you the way a mother cares for her children. We loved you dearly. Not content to just pass on the Message, we wanted to give you our hearts. And we did.[48]

The *New International Version* of the Bible renders the last sentence of that passage like this: "We loved you so much that we were delighted to share with you not only the gospel of God but our lives as well, because you had become so dear to us."[49]

Chew on Paul's phrasing for a moment. "We were delighted to share with you not only the gospel of God but our lives as well." "We shared the Gospel, but we shared our very lives, too." That was Paul's method. Sharing his very life with others.

It is also the way of Jesus, who loved us so much that he did not only give us a message, but he gave us himself. He shared not only the gospel of God, but his life as well.

Salt of the Earth

Jesus told his followers, "You are the salt of the earth."[50]

If you've been around the church for long, you've probably heard that statement a thousand times. Even if you're new to the church and the gospel, you're probably familiar with the phrase. But have you ever paused to think about *what it means*?

Salt gets into the thing it salts.

Just as the Word took on flesh and lived among us, salt must get into whatever it seasons or preserves. Salt doesn't sit up on the shelf and say, "Hey! You down there! Dude, you're going to hell!"

You'll never see a block of salt on the street corner handing out tracts. You'll never come across a saltshaker preaching with a loudspeaker on a street corner. I'm being silly, of course, but I think you get my point.

Salt must give itself to the thing it hopes to save or season.

And so must we.

Living the Revolution

Paul used a different analogy in 2 Corinthians 5:20, but it is also a revealing word picture if we stop to think about it: "We are Christ's ambassadors, and God is using us to speak to you."[51]

I'm sure I've read that verse hundreds of times, without taking the trouble to think much about it. But in Paul's day, no less than in ours, ambassadors didn't stay in Rome and hang out with the emperor; they went and lived among the people they were sent to. The really good ones learned to speak the same language and eat the same food as the people they were sent to. They didn't just share words. They moved into the neighborhood. They set up housekeeping. They *shared their lives* with the people they were sent to (at least, the *effective* ones did).

Mike Erre reminds every one of us that, if you are a Christ-follower:

You are not only a priest with a spiritual calling to ministry (in whatever you do), but also a full-time missionary whose job it is to put the message of Jesus on display by how you live. Many times we are called to use words in doing this, but often it is simply a matter of living the revolution. You don't need special training for this (though it would never hurt us); you need only the grace and power of God's Spirit within you and the courageous willingness to engage those people God puts around you. Remember, people can't help but talk about what they love and enjoy in life, whether it is a car, job, relationship, or hobby. If someone is passionate about the environment, I can't talk to that person for very long without hearing about it. If one of my single friends has a new girlfriend, I don't have to ask many questions in order to find out about her. Why is it any different [for] a person who is passionate for Jesus? Why do so many approaches to "sharing our faith" seem so awkward and contrived? Could it be because, instead of sharing our faith, we should just be sharing our lives—of which our faith is the defining part?[52]

Makes sense, right? Sounds good, sure. But how do we do that?

How to Share Your Life

In practical terms, what does it look like to share your life with others?

Be a Friend

Well, first, I think we've got to get intentional about spending time and living life with people who haven't experienced new life in Christ. Most people who have been in and around the church for any length of time live in a Christian ghetto of our own making. We schedule ourselves day after day with church activities until all of our friends are Christians. We spend time only with Christians. We barely know anyone who isn't a Christian. And believe it or not, that's not a good thing.

If you take a close look at the first chapters of the book of Acts, you'll see that in its earliest days, the first church—the church in Jerusalem—was settling in. They were having church; they were meeting in small groups; they were praying together, eating together, and helping each other out. And some preachers and scholars look at that picture (particularly in the latter verses of Acts 2) and see a picture of an ideal church. But I don't see it that way. Because if it was ideal, God wouldn't have had to change a thing. But he did.

If you continue reading past chapter two of Acts, all the way into chapter eight, you'll read the description of a "great persecution" that broke out against the church at Jerusalem. Those first followers of Jesus were hunted and jailed. And all but the leaders in the church were "scattered throughout the regions of Judea and Samaria."[53]

Why would God allow such a thing to happen? Especially when everything was going so well? I think the answer is this: God doesn't want his people living in a safe, comfortable little "bubble."

He wants us to get into the world around us. He doesn't want us spending our time *only* with other Christ-followers. We need strong, supportive relationships with other Christ-followers, but if the *only* people we ever hang out with are other Christ-followers, we are not living out the kind of concern for the world around us God wants to see in our lives.

We may say we love people who are far from God. But when we are actually faced with someone whose life is awfully messy, whose beliefs are thoroughly confused, and whose language or lifestyle is kinda rough, we may find it easy to get uncomfortable or offended, and we may end up doing something judgmental or looking for the quickest off-ramp in the relationship.

But the way of Jesus is exactly the opposite. He wove tales about seeking out lost sheep. He modeled a lifestyle of looking for such people. He talked about leaving the ninety-nine in the sheepfold and *prioritizing* the wayward one.

I truly believe Jesus wants us to be like him. He wants us to risk our reputations. He wants us to earn criticism from religious folk. He wants us to eat and drink with tax collectors and "sinners." He wants us to get out of our tidy Christian ghetto and hang out with people who are far from God . . . not to judge them, not to demand some Christian standard of behavior from them, not to look down our noses at them, but to actually and really be their friends, accepting them, relating to them, expressing genuine interest in what they think and what they enjoy, and not trying to squeeze them into *our* mold, but sharing our lives with them.

In fact, I think one of the worst things we do is try to convert someone we haven't tried to love yet. We try to persuade people to believe when we haven't gotten to know them, understand them, care about them, respect them, and all that goes with it.

Of course, there are exceptions. There are times when people cross our paths and the Spirit of God shows up and gives us just the right thing to say at just the right time. But I truly think our communities and our churches—and our lives—will be transformed if we break out of our Christian ghettoes and get to know our neighbors and coworkers and invite people to cookouts or parties, concerts and plays, who aren't already Christ-followers. (I'll say more about this in Chapter Nine.) And not just once in a while, either, but for the long haul.

Please don't misunderstand. I am not suggesting that we befriend people in order to "witness" to them. That is not "sharing our lives."

That is false friendship and not at all a reflection of what Jesus did. Steve McVey, president of Grace Walk Ministries, writes in his book *52 Lies Heard in Church Every Sunday*:

> Don't love people with an ulterior motive in mind. Let's just love people. After all, that's who you are! The truth is, if you befriend somebody only for the purpose of bringing them to faith in Christ, people sense it. They tend to know when we have a hidden agenda that we're not telling them. So let's set that aside and love folks because Christ in us does. God is love, and when we get in touch with our authentic selves, we'll see that our desire is to love people too.[54]

Sure, it may require a change in our schedules. We may be forced to cut back on the amount of time we spend inside a church building. The choir director may not be happy with you. The volunteer coordinator may call you a name. But that's a fair trade for the angelic rejoicing when a single lost soul is found because someone who loved God shared his or her life with a neighbor.

Be a Servant

Here's another way to share your life with others: look for ways to serve them.

When Jesus sent his twelve closest disciples two by two into the towns of Galilee and Judea to spread the good news of the kingdom, he told them: "Heal the sick, raise the dead, cleanse those who have leprosy, drive out demons. Freely you have received, freely give."[55]

In other words, they were giving value back to the community. In a big way. Rob Bell, founding pastor of Mars Hill Church in Grandville, Michigan, writes, "The most powerful things happen when the church surrenders its desire to convert people and convince them to join. It is when the church gives itself away in radical acts of service and compassion, expecting nothing in return, that the way of Jesus is most vividly on display."[56]

Some of the most fun I've ever had—honest—has been giving stuff away to people who didn't expect it (or understand it). Some of my happiest moments have been treating inner-city kids to a day at Sea World, or surprising a neighbor I saw in Bob Evans by paying for their lunch.

But sharing your life with others amounts to more than that. It involves being humble enough to—sometimes—let *them* serve *you*. We even see that in the Gospel of Matthew, as Jesus instructed the Twelve to give others a chance to help *them*. He said, "Whatever town or village you enter, search for some worthy person there and stay at his house until you leave."[57]

In other words, Jesus was saying, "Do what I did for Zacchaeus." He was saying, "Do what I did for the woman at the well, when I asked her for a drink of water. Share water with them, share a meal with them, share a home with them, share your life with them."

Be Yourself

When we begin to share our lives with people who are far from God, one of two extremes often happens. In some cases, we get so anxious to "share our faith" with a skeptic or seeker, we are constantly on pins and needles, wondering if *this* is the right moment, or if *that* was the right moment. And sometimes, instead of relaxing into a genuine, growing relationship, we become so intent on helping things along, so to speak, that our friend starts to feel like a "target" or a "project." No one likes that feeling.

Just as often, though, the opposite happens. Our relationship progresses and time passes, but we've never mentioned our faith. And the more time passes, the less comfortable we feel talking about our life of faith. Eventually, we kind of go into avoidance mode, because we're embarrassed for not having talked about it *before now.*

Oh, brother. It shouldn't be so hard. And it isn't, if we will just be ourselves and relate openly and honestly with a person from the very first moments in the relationship—not hiding anything, but not forcing anything, either.

For example, I have never yet met somebody who was insulted when they expressed a need and I told them I'd pray for them. I've never had anybody get offended by that.

It's a simple thing, but I don't know why it so seldom occurs to us to relate to skeptics and seekers like we relate to each other. I'm not talking about tossing around a lot of "Praise Gods" and "Hallelujahs" and "God told me you're the person I'm gonna marry!" (Those are not usually big relationship builders.) I just mean saying things like, "I just heard a song that moved me to tears. Do you want to hear it?" or "A friend said something at church yesterday that really made sense to me," or something like that.

It's not the Four Spiritual Laws; it's just being *you* and speaking what's on your mind and in your heart. Which is where we usually mess up anyway when it comes to sharing our faith. Skeptics and seekers can smell a fake a mile away, but a little openness about spiritual things goes a long way.

So again, I say to you: quit sharing your faith. Share your life instead. Make space in your life for people who seem far from God. Find ways to serve them. And just be yourself. You might be surprised at how God moves, not only in your friends, but in you.

~~୬ *Prayer*

Lord God Adonai, thank you for the life you have given me, by grace through faith in Jesus, your Son. Forgive me for seeing others as "targets" or "projects." Forgive me for being judgmental, patronizing, or condescending toward those you are seeking. Forgive me for being too busy or careless to share my life with people outside the church. I repent, and I thank you for your forgiveness and cleansing.

Teach me to share my life with those around me—neighbors, coworkers, customers, and so on. Help me to broaden my horizons and get to know more and more people who haven't yet experienced new life in Christ. Show me how my attitude needs to improve, where my schedule needs to change, and to whom my focus and friendship needs to turn, starting now, in Jesus' name. Amen.

CHAPTER FIVE

Quit Tithing

Money is a ticklish subject in the church. And outside the church, too. Pretty much everywhere and in almost any situation.

Talking about money makes people nervous. Sociologist Robert Wuthnow considers the subject of money "the darkest taboo in our culture."[58] Which certainly says something about us, and our attitudes. And maybe even our affections.

Money is a sensitive topic for any number of reasons. We're embarrassed because we have more of it than others do. Or because we have less than others. Or because we give less than others do. Or because we don't want to part with it. In each case, however, it makes us uncomfortable because, one way or another, it means too much to us. And, whether we have plenty or not enough—or what we think is not enough—it sometimes means so much to us it gets in the way.

As a pastor, I have always approached the topic of money—and giving—carefully. Partly because I'm a nice guy; I don't like to make people uncomfortable. I also know that, in the eyes of some people, a pastor who preaches on giving can sound self-serving, like a congressman who votes to raise congressional salaries. But I also tend to tread lightly on the subject because I know that many people—churchgoers and nonchurchgoers alike—are inclined to believe that churches just want their money, and preaching or teaching on giving merely confirms their suspicions. For all those reasons, I tried to seize every opportunity to surprise and counteract people's expectations.

One particular Sunday, instead of taking an offering, the ushers passed out money during our morning worship services. (We didn't advertise our plans ahead of time, though. If we had, we probably would have broken attendance records.) We asked each worshipper to take rather than give that morning; each offering bag was stuffed with envelopes of money. Some envelopes had five dollars, others ten dollars, and some twenty dollars. We told everyone they were free to spend the amount they received, save it, pay bills with it, invest it, or return it, asking only that they let us know the impact the funds had on them or someone else.

Another time, we included a dollar bill in every program that was handed out to worshippers as they entered for worship that day. There was no explanation. Just a dollar bill among other program inserts. Then, during the morning's sermon, I mentioned the dollar and asked them to hold it in their hands for a few moments. I said, "Do you know 1.2 billion people in the world survive on one dollar a day . . . or less? You hold in your hand a whole day's wages to many of the people in this world. And yet we are so incredibly wealthy that we are given a dollar, absolutely free, and for most of us it doesn't even warrant a *thank you*.

Do you see how rich we've become? Food, clothes, cars, houses, jewelry, furniture, electronics, you name it. A dollar is nothing compared to all that. It won't even buy something at the Dollar Store, because we need a few cents more to pay the sales tax. Yet to 1.2 billion people in the world, it would be a windfall."

I have also frequently instructed visitors and guests in our worship services not to participate in the offering but to allow the church to serve them without any sense of obligation on their part. Numerous people have told me they were surprised—and even moved to generosity—by that announcement.

So let me assure you. I understand what a touchy subject money is for most of us. So relax. I'm not going to tell you that you should tithe. In fact, quite the opposite.

I'm going to suggest that you quit tithing.

A Time-Honored Practice

I believe money—and tithing in particular—is an area in which a great deal of how we believe and behave as churchgoing people bears little resemblance to the way of Jesus. It is an area in which I think we have strayed far from the way things are meant to be in the kingdom of God.

Of course, you may not quite know what I'm talking about. If you're not accustomed to the way church people talk, you may be unfamiliar with the word *tithe*, or the concept of a tithe. It is basically just an old-fashioned word for "tenth." A tithe is a tenth of something.

There's an incident recorded in Genesis, the first book of the Bible. Abram, who would become the father of all the Jewish people, heard that his nephew, Lot, had been taken prisoner during a regional war. So Abram, a wealthy and powerful man in that region, set out to rescue his nephew, which he did, rescuing also the rest of the people—and their goods—who had been taken captive along with Lot.

On his return, as Abram marched triumphantly home with a caravan of rescued people and reclaimed booty, he was greeted by Melchizedek, a mysterious figure the Bible identifies as the "king of Jerusalem" and "priest of God Most High." The Bible says, "Then Abram gave him [Melchizedek] a tenth of everything" (Gen. 14:20b).

That might have meant that Abram recognized Melchizedek as a representative of God, and so he gave ten percent of the spoils to Melchizedek as a way of saying thank you to God.

Years later, when God had delivered the Jewish people from slavery in Egypt and established them as a brand-new nation, he worked through a man named Moses to establish a whole new set of laws, customs, and procedures for these several million former slaves.

One of the laws he established was, "A tithe of everything from the land, whether grain from the soil or fruit from the trees, belongs to the LORD; it is holy to the LORD. . . . The entire tithe of the herd and flock—every tenth animal that passes under the shepherd's rod—will be holy to the LORD. He must not pick out the good from the bad or make any substitution."[59]

In other words, since these people had been redeemed out of slavery by God, since they claimed to worship God, they were commanded to give a tenth of their crops and their flocks as a tithe to the Lord.

Thus, at various times throughout history, the tithe has been the accepted standard of giving and gratitude for those who worship God. Giving a tenth of your income, your prosperity, your goods toward the work of God is a time-honored practice throughout church history.

But I'm here to tell you today: if you *have* been tithing, if you *have* been giving ten percent of your income to the local church, to the work of God in your community, stop it.

Quit tithing.

If you haven't been tithing, don't start.

And I'm not kidding.

Just the Beginning

Listen, I know a lot of pastors and church leaders emphasize the tithe, and they preach and pray and coax and cajole and hope and wish that their church members would start to give a tithe so that the work of the church can move forward, so that needs can be met, so that positions can be filled, and so on and so forth.

Been there. Done that.

And believe me, there is no doubt that if every churchgoer in your community were to give ten percent of his or her income to the church, it would turn that community upside down in no time at all. In fact, it has been estimated that if every churchgoer tithed, the church could reach out in such a way as to make government welfare obsolete and poverty disappear. What's not to love about that?

In spite of the statistics, however, I tell you from my heart—and I believe I am telling you in Jesus' name—that you can quit tithing, and you can quit now.

In fact, it would be best if you did.

You see, the tithe was a requirement of the law God gave to his people through Moses. And ten percent was just the beginning.

Every year, a Jew gave ten percent of his crops, his produce, and his flocks to what was called the "Levite's Tithe," to support the temple worship system that was the center of the religious life of Israel. There were twenty-four different orders of priests, with thousands upon thousands of priests who kept the temple running.

But the priests were more than that, because Israel was a theocracy. So the temple officials were literally government officials; they were the legislative branch, the executive branch, and the judicial branch all rolled into one. So the "Levite's Tithe" was actually a tax that kept not only the religious life but also the civic life of the nation running.

But it didn't stop there. In addition to the "Levite's Tithe," a Jewish head-of-household gave another ten percent every year, which funded all the religious feasts and national convocations—the feast of Firstfruits, the feast of Pentecost, the feast of Trumpets, the feast of Tabernacles, and on and on, along with the holy days, the Sabbaths, and more.

So that's a tithe to the Levites and a tithe to support all the festivals, *and then* there was another tithe that was paid every third year, which went to the poor and the widows . . . sort of a combination of welfare and social security tax.

So if you break all that down, the average Jew "tithed" about twenty-three percent of his income a year to a system of taxation to fund the religious, civic, and charitable life of the nation. Thus, if you want to tithe like Old Testament Jews tithed, then your starting point is not ten percent. It's more like twenty-three percent.

And that's not to mention that you would also owe a half-shekel temple tax every year, and if you had a field, you had to harvest the field in a circular pattern so as to leave the crop in the corners unharvested and available to the poor (a practice which played a role in the Old Testament story of Ruth and her eventual marriage to Boaz). Oh, and if a bale of hay happened to tumble off your wagon on the way to the barn, you had to leave it—again for the poor.

Start adding all that up, and you're getting close to twenty-five percent of your income.

What Is God's?

When you get into the Christian Scriptures, what folks call the New
Testament, all this was still going on to some extent. Even though Israel
was an occupied nation, they still had the temple to support, schools to
fund, festivals to hold, and courts to maintain.

That's why the question the Pharisees put to Jesus about paying taxes
to Rome was so inflammatory, because the Jews were still paying all their
tithes and *on top of that*, along came Rome, which said, "You need to support Rome, too."

But Jesus answered their tricky question by asking his questioners for
a coin—which was stamped with the image of the emperor—and saying,
"Give to Caesar what is Caesar's, and to God what is God's."[60] It was a
clever rejoinder, a typical "Jesus response" to a rhetorical trap that had
been laid for him. His response neatly avoided the thorny political and
economic issues while focusing instead on that which is most important
to Jesus . . . and that which should be most important to his true followers.

Jesus' answer to the Pharisees cut to the heart of the matter. As
Jesus often did, however, he introduced a new question, a more search-
ing conundrum. And that is: What *is* God's?

In other words, the Old Testament obligation to tithe tells us that
ten percent—the firstfruits—of everything we have belongs to God. Jesus
says something different. Way different. Exponentially different. He tells
us that *one hundred percent*—the whole enchilada—of everything we have
belongs to God.

You see, the way of Jesus is *not* the way of ten percent. The way of
Jesus is the way of *one hundred percent.*

He said, "You cannot become my disciple without giving up everything you own."[61] That may not be the best witnessing verse, but there it is. If you call yourself a Christ-follower and believe or behave as if what you own or earn belongs to you, then Jesus says, "I'm sorry; that's not what I expect of my followers."

One hundred percent is the way of Jesus.

It is the way of his kingdom.

The One Hundred Percent Way

One day in the temple, "Jesus saw the rich putting their gifts into the temple treasury. He also saw a poor widow put in two very small copper coins. 'I tell you the truth,' he said, 'this poor widow has put in more than all the others. All these people gave their gifts out of their wealth; but she out of her poverty put in all she had to live on.'"[62]

This is the language of Jesus.

Everything.

All.

A rich young man once came to him, asking what he must do to inherit eternal life, and Jesus said, "Sell everything you have and give to the poor, and you will have treasure in heaven. Then come, follow me."[63]

The way of Jesus is *not* the way of ten percent. It is the way of *one hundred percent.*

Managers, Not Owners

You see, the ancients understood something that we do not. When the tithe was instituted, the practice God prescribed was *not* that of giving God a bull, a fattened calf, or the firstfruits of the fields and keeping the rest. The idea was that because God owns everything, each man gave him the first part of everything as a way of acknowledging his ownership and as a way of expressing gratitude for the portion God had entrusted to his care. In other words, he brought to him the firstfruits, his best bull, his ten percent, to represent all the rest—one hundred percent.

As Andy Stanley writes in his book *Enemies of the Heart*:

> If we're going to leave it all behind when we die, then one thing's abundantly clear: We're not owners; we're managers. Some people get to manage more than others, but none of us are owners. . . .
>
> The truth is, God owns everything. King David acknowledged this. For King *Anybody* to acknowledge that God is the owner of everything is unusual. But in David's day, it was generally accepted that the king owned everything and everybody in his realm. But David knew better. He said:
>
> Yours, Lord, is the greatness and the power
> and the glory and the majesty and the splendor,
> for everything in heaven and earth is yours.
> Yours, Lord, is the kingdom;
> you are exalted as head over all (1 Chronicles 29:11).[64]

King David's perspective is drastically different from our modern mindset. We live in what has been dubbed an "ownership society." The concept goes beyond ownership of personal assets, but it includes them. And its acceptance and prevalence in our lives may show how far today's Christ-followers have come from the first-century church.

First, Not Final

The Bible says, "The law was our schoolmaster to bring us unto Christ, that we might be justified by faith. But after that faith is come, we are no longer under a schoolmaster."[65] What if the Old Testament tithe, the idea of giving ten percent, was intended to *tutor* us in stewardship, to *train* God's people to acknowledge God as the owner of everything and learn to be generous and giving and gracious with *all* his gifts to us? What if the tithe was not intended to be the limit for managers of God's resources, but merely the first lessons in stewardship?

It certainly seems as though it looked that way in the first years of the church. Luke, the author of the book of Acts, reported: "All the believers were together and had everything in common. Selling their possessions and goods, they gave to anyone as he had need."[66]

And, if we missed it the first time, he reiterates two chapters later: "All the believers were one in heart and mind. No one claimed that any of his possessions was his own, but they shared everything they had."[67]

These descriptions of the first group of Christ-followers have been sometimes misread as an endorsement of socialism. On the contrary, I believe they depict the graduation of early Christians from "tithing school." They show a group of people who had grasped the way of Jesus—the one hundred percent way.

The "Five-Way" Way of Life

I've lived most of my life in and around Cincinnati, Ohio. One of many local delicacies in this area is "Cincinnati chili." It is a combination of spaghetti, uniquely spiced chili, and other ingredients in various combinations: kidney beans, diced onion, and finely grated cheese. A plate of spaghetti and chili is called a "two-way." Adding the grated cheese makes it a "three-way." And the beans and onions create a "four-way" and "five-way." I've even heard that one establishment in the area has long offered a "six-way," topping a five-way with a fried egg. (I'm not particularly anxious to try that concoction.)

Take my word for it: a Cincinnati chili four-way or five-way is better than it sounds. And so it is with the way of Jesus. The Christ-follower who graduates from "tithing school" to the one hundred percent way will experience a way of life far beyond that of the ten percent way. It is an exponential improvement over the schoolmaster from whom some of us learned about money and giving. The way of Jesus contrasts with the tithe in four other ways.

The Way of Freedom and Joy

The way of the tithe is the way of obligation. When a man or woman gives the required tithe, his or her duty is done, the vow fulfilled, and the responsibility discharged. But the way of Jesus is the way of freedom and joy.

He says, "Freely you have received, freely give."[68] And Paul told the Christ-followers living in Corinth: "Each man should give what he has decided in his heart to give, not reluctantly or under compulsion, for God loves a cheerful giver."[69]

The way of Jesus is the way of freedom and joy. No accountant is needed. There are no receipts to save. We are free to give—and give—until it brings a smile to our faces and laughter to our hearts.

The Way of Greater Faith

The way of the tithe is a way of faith, believing that God has given you what you have. But the way of Jesus is the way of greater faith, believing that God is big enough, faithful enough, and generous enough to provide for you *tomorrow* so that you can be as magnanimous as you want to be *today*.

To quote Paul again:

Remember this: Whoever sows sparingly will also reap sparingly, and whoever sows generously will also reap generously.... And God is able to make all grace abound to you, so that in all things at all times, having all that you need, you will abound in every good work. As it is written:

> "He has scattered abroad his gifts to the poor;
>   his righteousness endures forever."

Now he who supplies seed to the sower and bread for food will also supply and increase your store of seed and will enlarge the harvest of your righteousness. You will be made rich in every way so that you can be generous on every occasion, and through us your generosity will result in thanksgiving to God.[70]

The way of Jesus promotes generosity because God is able to supply—or resupply—all our needs.

The Way of Abundance

The way of the tithe is the way of scarcity; that is, there's only so much to go around, so I give God what I owe him and make the rest stretch as far as I can. But the way of Jesus is the way of abundance, believing that whatever riches God sends my way are given to me so that I can be generous.

That's what is so wrong, so unbiblical, and so un-Christlike about the "health and wealth" gospel, the self-indulgent crap that some preachers and televangelists preach, that says we should *give* more and more so that we will *get* more and more.

That's exactly backwards.

Yes, Paul says, "If you sow generously, you'll reap generously," *but* he goes on to say,

"You will be made rich in every way *so that* you can be generous on every occasion."[71] This verse seems to say that, if God prospers you, he prospers you not so you can be rich, but rather so you can be generous. That is totally in keeping with the way God's kingdom operates: when he blesses a man, a woman, a church, or a nation, he blesses them so they can be a blessing to others. That principle was at the heart of God's promise to Abraham: "I will surely bless you and make your descendants as numerous as the stars in the sky and as the sand on the seashore. . . . [T]hrough your offspring all nations on earth will be blessed."[72]

This principle is at the heart of the gospel, as well, for everyone who is called into the kingdom of light is also called to let that light shine before others.[73]

The Way of Impossibilities

The way of the tithe is the way of possibilities; that is, my giving to God is always in proportion to how well I'm doing. But the way of Jesus, the way of God's kingdom, is the way of *im*possibilities, making it possible for me to give *beyond* what is possible.

Paul referred to this paradox when he commended the generosity of the Macedonian churches: "And now, brothers, we want you to know about the grace that God has given the Macedonian churches. Out of the most severe trial, their overflowing joy and their extreme poverty welled up in rich generosity. For I testify that they gave as much as they were able, and even beyond their ability."[74]

What's that again? How is it possible to give *beyond* your ability? How is it possible for "extreme poverty" to produce "rich generosity?" It's not; it's *not* possible at all. And yet it happened. And it still happens today. With God all things are possible.

The Macedonian churches gave beyond their ability. The widow in the temple gave more than all the rich folk combined. The impossible becomes possible when you quit tithing . . . and start distributing God's resources—the one hundred percent that belongs to him—in faith, freely, generously, cheerfully, abundantly, courageously, even impossibly.

Does that mean you rip up your tithe check and sell a field instead (as Barnabas did, as Acts 4:36–37 records)? Maybe. Does it mean you empty your piggy bank, as the widow in the temple did? Could be. Does it mean you change your lifestyle? Drain your bank accounts? Sell all you have? Possibly.

But maybe not. I mean, how are you supposed to know? Ten percent was a pretty good benchmark—until you read this chapter, right? So what do you do now?

Well, since I've already referred several times to 2 Corinthians 8 and 9, let me conclude by suggesting that if you love God, if you follow Christ, if you want nothing more than to make your Father happy and make him a "proud Papa," then you might prayerfully ask yourself ten questions about how you give to God and his kingdom, the needs of people around you, and the work of your church as well as other groups that minister around the world.

These questions are drawn primarily from Paul's words to the church at Corinth, two thousand years ago, but I believe they represent the way of Jesus and the way of God's kingdom far, far better than the Old Testament tithe.

1. Does my giving reflect God's ownership of everything I own or earn? (2 Cor. 8:5; Luke 14:33)
2. Am I giving in an attitude of grace and freedom or out of legalism and obligation? (2 Cor. 8:1, 9:7; Matt. 10:8)

3. Am I giving as an expression of sincere love for God and others? (2 Cor. 8:9)
4. Am I giving in response to Christ's inexpressible gift? (2 Cor. 8:9, 9:15)
5. Am I giving out of a sincere desire? (2 Cor. 8:8, 10, 12, 9:7)
6. Am I following through and keeping promises? (2 Cor. 8:10–12)
7. Am I giving cheerfully, not reluctantly or under compulsion? (2 Cor. 9:5, 7, 9)
8. Am I giving only "according to my means," or am I learning to give "beyond my (apparent) ability?" (2 Cor. 8:3)
9. Is my giving a good example to others? (2 Cor. 9:2, 11–12)
10. Does my giving reflect the belief that "God is able to make all grace abound to me" and "supply and multiply [my] seed for sowing and increase the harvest of [my] righteousness"? (2 Cor. 9:6, 8, 10–11)

If those questions reveal a "one hundred percent heart," then be encouraged. Rejoice! Give thanks. If, on the other hand, they spotlight some areas in which there is room for improvement, then pray. Ask God to further transform you into the likeness of Christ and the one hundred percent way of his kingdom.

~⚘ *Prayer*

Gracious Father, you have freely given me countless good and perfect gifts,[75] *for which I give you thanks: life, breath, forgiveness, food, clothes, cars, home, family, faith, laughter, and more. Make me truly grateful for these and all your generous gifts.*

Teach me a new way of life, a "Jesus way of life." Help me to "graduate" from law and operate instead by grace through faith. Let my attitude toward money and possessions reflect your ownership of everything I have. Let me leave behind the "ten percent way" of obligation, faith, scarcity, and possibilities, and follow instead the "hundred percent way" of Jesus. Make me loving, sincere, and generous with all you have given me, not claiming that any of my possessions are my own. Cultivate in me the grace of giving, that I may give according to your *ability and not my own, in Jesus' name. Amen.*

CHAPTER SIX

Quit Volunteering

I quit.

I've spent most of thirty-plus years trying to get people to volunteer. As a pastor and church leader, I've begged. I've pleaded. I've cajoled. I've conspired. I've preached on serving. I've tried to set an example. I've been a part of "service fairs," where people could go from one fun booth to another, playing games and meeting folks and—we hoped—signing up to do something. I've had ushers hand out sign-up forms and threatened not to dismiss the congregation until enough people had signed up to serve in the church nursery.

And most of it had very little effect.

Don't get the wrong idea. I've served alongside some of the greatest servants in the world. I don't have the words to adequately praise people like Doug and Stella, who drove a van through crime-ridden neighborhoods to get scores of children to church. I can't possibly say too much about volunteers like John and Bill and Daryl, who would leave home before 6:30 A.M. to tow a twenty-four-foot trailer to a middle school so they and others could set up a portable church in time for a 9 A.M. service. There is no way I can express my appreciation for Barb, who served as a nursery worker, teacher of teens, leader of women, cooker of meals, driver of vans, and more. I could go on.

But like nearly every pastor on the face of the earth, I watched week after week, year after year, as roughly twenty percent of the people did eighty percent—or more—of the work. The situation is so widespread, I'm tempted to say, "Show me a church that isn't chronically short on volunteers, and I'll show you a church that is chronically short on vision."

And, to be honest, I'm sick of it. So I quit. I won't ask you to volunteer. In fact, I'll do more than that: I'll tell you not to. Please.

A Time-Honored Practice

For two thousand years now, the church has been built on ground that is soaked with the blood of martyrs—and the sweat of servants. There is not a church in the world that can function without multiple levels of volunteer effort.

Nursery workers.

Musicians.

Teachers.

Ushers.

Cooks.

Chaperones.

Greeters.

Window washers.

Drivers.

Treasurers.

Prayer warriors.

Bookkeepers.

Receptionists.

Lawn mowers.

Parking lot attendants.

Sound techs.

Gardeners.

Leaders.

And more. All of these roles are crucial. But none of them should be filled with mere volunteers.

A Gift-Based Organism

The written history of the early church relates an incident that should inform the way we do things as followers of Jesus—but it seldom does.

The number of followers was growing. But during this same time, the Greek-speaking followers had an argument with the other followers. The Greek-speaking widows were not getting their share of the food that was given out every day. The twelve apostles called the whole group of followers together and said, "It is not right for us to stop our work of teaching God's word in order to serve tables. So, brothers and sisters, choose seven of your own men who are good, full of the Spirit and full of wisdom. We will put them in charge of this work. Then we can continue to pray and to teach the word of God."

The whole group liked the idea, so they chose these seven men: Stephen (a man with great faith and full of the Holy Spirit), Philip, Procorus, Nicanor, Timon, Parmenas, and Nicolas (a man from Antioch who had become a follower of the Jewish religion). Then they put these men before the apostles, who prayed and laid their hands on them.

The word of God was continuing to spread. The group of followers in Jerusalem increased, and a great number of the Jewish priests believed and obeyed.[76]

Notice what these verses say—and don't say. They don't describe a "ministry fair." They don't mention passionate pleas from the pulpit. They don't describe any high-pressure sales tactics. But they do show a group of leaders who were keenly aware of both their place and their purpose. They reasoned, "It is not right for us to stop our work of teaching God's word in order to serve tables." Or, as *The Message* paraphrase puts it, "It wouldn't be right for us to abandon our responsibilities for preaching and teaching the Word of God to help with the care of the poor."[77] Stop for a moment. Think about those words. "It wouldn't be right?" Really? Why not?

Well, at first glance, it might look or sound like the church's leaders were a bit arrogant—too good, maybe, to stoop so low as to wait tables. But that's not it at all.

Notice also that they didn't say, "It wouldn't be convenient," or "It wouldn't be advantageous." No, they said, "It is not right for us to stop our work of teaching God's word in order to serve tables."

There is something remarkable in there. Something we routinely miss. In our twenty-first century attitudes and actions as churchgoing people, I think we have strayed from the way things are meant to be. Those first-century church leaders seem utterly assured of their place and purpose in the church. They were devoted to teaching and preaching. That's half of the story.

The other half of the story is that those leaders apparently also had a strong sense that many others in the church possessed a different place and purpose from themselves. They put out the word for seven men who were "good, full of the Spirit and full of wisdom" to take on this new role. In other words, they were sure there had to be a sufficient number of people who were uniquely graced and gifted to meet the needs that had arisen.

The Bible makes it clear that the church is intended to be a gift-driven organism, *not* a volunteer-driven organization. Back when the church was enlisting the efforts of "the Seven" in the critical ministry of caring for the widows, a man named Saul was doing everything he could to destroy the church. When one of those seven men became the first martyr of the young church, Saul was among his executioners.[78] But before long, of course, Saul met the risen Christ on the road to Damascus and became the greatest church planter of the first century. That man, who became better known as Paul the Apostle, emphasized this gift-driven dynamic on many occasions. In his letter to the church at Rome, he wrote:

> God in his kindness gave each of us different gifts. If your gift is speaking God's word, make sure what you say agrees with the Christian faith. If your gift is serving, then devote yourself to serving. If it is teaching, devote yourself to teaching. If it is encouraging others, devote yourself to giving encouragement. If it is sharing, be generous. If it is leadership, lead enthusiastically. If it is helping people in need, help them cheerfully.[79]

Consider how Paul could have written those lines. He could have said, "God wants each of us to volunteer everywhere we can. If you want to preach, sign up. If you want to sing, try out. If you want to lead, step forward." And so on. But he didn't, of course. Because the church is not the Rotary Club or the hospital auxiliary. It is an organism, comprised of people with different gifts and abilities. Even the smallest congregation should not be assembled haphazardly, according to who volunteers for this or that; it is already assembled. Its members simply need to discover their purpose and place and begin exercising their God-given gifts *there*.

So I think the Twelve said those words—"It wouldn't be right"—for two reasons: first, because it wouldn't be right for them to abandon *their* place and purpose, and, second, because it wouldn't be right for them to prevent other people from discovering *their* place and purpose. If the leaders had given a different answer, that first-century Jerusalem church would have been doubly impoverished. Like many of our churches today.

Beauty and Blessedness

There is within each of us a longing to be useful, to be needed, to contribute to the lives of others in a meaningful way; we have a desire to know that we've made a difference to someone, a hunger to be a part of something important, worthwhile, or even great.

You've felt it, haven't you?

Maybe you're even feeling it now.

We all long to fit in somewhere and to believe that we're important, that we have something to offer, that we're not insignificant, but that somewhere there is a place, a role, a function where we can fit in and do something valuable and fulfilling. I believe that desire can be—*must* be—met in and through our experience of community in the life of the church, the Body of Christ. But the way we fill roles and offices in the church is usually something paltry and pitiful. And it exposes our own willingness to settle for busyness when we should settle for nothing short of beauty and blessedness.

Picture yourself entering a vast concert hall. Before you on the stage sits an orchestra, a complex jumble of stringed instruments, brass instruments, percussion instruments, and woodwinds. Their sizes, shapes, and colors couldn't be more different. The piano and the piccolo. The trumpet and the timpani. The harp and the oboe. The violin and the xylophone.

You take your seat amid a cacophony of sound, each instrument bleating or blasting notes of its own. But soon the dissension quiets, and the cavernous room falls silent. A black-suited form enters from the wings, ascends a small platform, and lifts a thin baton into the air.

With a single downstroke, everything changes. All joining together, the harp and oboe, trumpet and timpani, piano and piccolo produce strains of music that delight your ears and lift your soul to ecstatic heights. Time stands still. You forget to breathe. Until the last note sounds, and the room erupts in grateful applause.

What just happened? How did it happen? None of those various instruments is capable—alone—of creating such a moment. Sure, a single sax player on a street corner or a gifted guitarist in a park can work wonders. But it takes much more to create a symphony of sound and emotion. Combine the crisp tones of a trumpet with the thunder of a tuba and the cascading notes of a harp, and *together* they wield an amazing power, a power *far beyond* the capabilities of a single instrument or any one musician.

That is the church. The church is an orchestra made up of a wide range of instruments played by a diverse array of musicians. And God himself selects who will play what. As the conductor, he determines the sections and then decides which part each will play. Because he is also the composer, the music he writes is perfectly suited to each member of the orchestra and perfectly designed to accomplish his purpose.

Every follower of Jesus—every person who has experienced salvation by trusting Christ and thus received new life by the power of God's Holy Spirit—is a member of that vast orchestra. And God has placed in your hands, whether you know it or not, an instrument that is perfectly suited to you. Not a trumpet. Nor a tuba. Another kind of instrument, the kind the Bible calls a "spiritual gift."

Gift Precedes Function

Around the same time he wrote about spiritual gifts to the church at Rome, Paul also wrote a series of letters to the church in Corinth, in which he presented a lengthy depiction of how each of us is intended to function in the church. He wrote, "Now about the gifts of the Spirit, brothers and sisters, I do not want you to be uninformed."[80]

Paul used that particular phrase—"I do not want you to be uninformed"—six times in his letters:

- Twice in reference to the Jewish people, whose disobedience brought judgment.
- Once in reference to his plans to visit the church at Rome.
- Once regarding the sufferings he and his team had endured throughout Asia.
- Once in reference to the end times and the resurrection of the dead.
- In 1 Corinthians 12:1, where he says, "I do not want you to be uninformed" about spiritual gifts.

Take a moment and think. What are the top five or six things you want your loved ones to know? What would you list, off the top of your head, as five or six ways you would complete the sentence, "I don't want you to be uninformed about . . ."? Would you list salvation? Sexual purity?

Money management? Something else? Whatever might be on your list, it is informative that Paul chose to emphasize an understanding of spiritual gifts and how important they are to the church.

He went on to write, "There are different kinds of gifts, but the same Spirit distributes them. There are different kinds of service, but the same Lord. There are different kinds of working, but in all of them and in everyone it is the same God at work."[81] Of all the things Paul thought important to write about, he not only mentioned but emphasized spiritual gifts—because those gifts God gives to his children are key to the proper functioning of the church, and to the fun and fulfillment your soul craves.

What Is a Spiritual Gift?

Paul provides a concise definition of spiritual gifts in verse 7 of his discourse in 1 Corinthians 12, when he says: "Now to each one the manifestation of the Spirit is given for the common good."

A spiritual gift is a manifestation of the Holy Spirit of God. When you become a Christian and receive the indwelling Spirit of God, he will manifest himself. And one of the ways he manifests himself is in the giving and working of spiritual gifts. This definition differentiates a spiritual gift from a natural gift or talent or skill; those things may interact with a spiritual gift, and spiritual gifts are often exercised in areas where a talent or skill already exists, but a spiritual gift is a manifestation of the Spirit. So, while it may look a lot like a talent or skill, a spiritual gift is much more than that.

Paul also says that these manifestations of the Spirit are given "to each one." That means that every Christian receives a spiritual gift. Some may receive more than one, but each one receives at least one. There is not a single Christian on the face of the earth who can say, "I don't have a spiritual gift." There is not a single Christian with any reason to feel cheated. There is no true follower of Jesus who has not been supernaturally enabled by God to do something important and valuable for the Body of Christ.

Paul also mentions the purpose of spiritual gifts: "for the common good." Spiritual gifts are not given to glorify you, to make you feel important, to make you better than someone else; they're given for the benefit of others, for the common good of the whole church.

That's one major difference between volunteerism and the way things are supposed to be done in the church. People volunteer for all kinds of reasons: they feel guilty, they want to impress someone, they long to be admired, and so on. And many churches struggle to grow and minister effectively because some people are "in it" for the wrong reasons, or in the wrong position. People can labor for years—decades, even—in volunteer roles for which they're unsuited and in which they're unhappy. That kind of situation can wreak havoc on a church. And it can do great harm to the person in that role as well as to the people with whom he or she interacts.

Charles Swindoll defines spiritual gifts as "Divinely-bestowed abilities or skills . . . which enable the believer to perform his or her function in the Body of Christ (universal Church) so that the Body functions with the maximum amount of effectiveness."[82] It is that enablement that makes fun and fulfillment possible. I believe when you're exercising your spiritual gift or gifts, you're more likely to be having a great time and more likely to feel fully alive and significant.

How Many Different Spiritual Gifts Are There?

Having just finished saying that "to each one the manifestation of the Spirit is given for the common good," Paul goes on:

To one there is given through the Spirit a message of wisdom, to another a message of knowledge by means of the same Spirit, to another faith by the same Spirit, to another gifts of healing by that one Spirit, to another miraculous powers, to another prophecy, to another distinguishing between spirits, to another speaking in different kinds of tongues, and to still another the interpretation of tongues.[83]

Paul says, basically, "there are all kinds of spiritual gifts," and he lists some of them here. We know he doesn't try to list them all, because elsewhere in his writings, he mentions more than the nine listed above. His other lists—in his letters to the Romans and the churches around Ephesus—include:

encouragement
leadership
pastoring
teaching
serving
evangelism
giving
showing mercy

And, since none of the gifts appear in every list, it is reasonable to believe that these are sample lists, and we might even infer that the Spirit may give a wider variety of gifts than the three Scriptural lists combined.[84] Maybe music composition, artistic expression, hospitality, or even an aptitude for creating PowerPoint presentations.

Who Gets What?

As he gets deeper into his discussion about spiritual gifts, Paul goes on to mention how they are distributed: "All these [that is, all these spiritual gifts] are the work of one and the same Spirit, and he distributes them to each one, just as he determines."[85]

The Spirit of God determines who gets what gift. Not you. Not me. Not any earthly authority. God himself, by his Spirit, decides who gets what gift. At the end of this twelfth chapter, Paul does say to "eagerly desire the greater gifts," but whether or not we have the gift of teaching or serving, leadership or showing mercy, is not determined by us, but by God and God alone.

You see, you can *learn* a skill, you can *acquire* a talent, but you're *given* a gift. Skills and talents may help you exercise your gift, and you can certainly learn to use your gift more and more effectively, but it's not something you can earn, and it's not something you can learn; it's something that is given to you by the Spirit.

So, if you are a Christ-follower, you *have* a spiritual gift. Right now. And it's a gift or gifts that the Spirit of God in his sovereign, infinite wisdom has chosen for you.

So you don't have to wonder if you have a gift. You don't even have to work hard in order to get it. You just have to identify it and begin to use it. You may already know what your spiritual gift is. You may have no idea. You may have suffered disappointment as a Christian because you've been trying to exercise some gift or gifts you don't possess, or you may already be using it without knowing what it's called.

But I'll tell you this: If you can know your spiritual gift or gifts and find a way to use them, you will experience a level of fun and fulfillment that may just blow your mind and lift your spiritual life to heights you didn't know were possible.

So how do you do that? How do you find your spiritual gift? There are four primary ways.

Prayer. Ask God to help you discern your spiritual gift. Make it an ongoing focus of your concerted prayer efforts.

Trial and error. Some people figure out their gift by trying this and trying that, until finally they hit on something that enables them to function "with ease and effectiveness" they never experienced before. The key, in this case, is not stopping or settling until you've found strong indications of your giftedness.

Observation and counsel. Ask mature Christians who know you what *they* think your spiritual gift is.

Assessment tools. Numerous spiritual gift assessments exist in books and workbooks. Many are available online. Keep in mind, though, that most will assist you in determining your spiritual gifts from the Bible lists; other possibilities (such as music) are seldom included in these assessments.

Place Follows Purpose

Once you have begun to understand and exercise your spiritual gift, you will probably begin to sense more clarity about the most fruitful, fun, and fulfilling places for you to serve the church.

A Place for You

In *West Side Story*, Leonard Bernstein's inspired adaptation of *Romeo and Juliet*, lovers Maria and Tony sing a hopeful song, "Somewhere (A Place for Us)," imagining a place where they could enjoy "peace and quiet and open air." Everyone hopes for that. The human heart was created to fit somewhere, to find a place where our lives and our efforts count for something.

The Bible assures us that such a place exists for each one of us. Paul goes on in 1 Corinthians 12 to set up a metaphor, which forms the basis of that promise: "Just as a body, though one, has many parts, but all its many parts form one body, so it is with Christ. For we were all baptized by one Spirit so as to form one body—whether Jews or Gentiles, slave or free—and we were all given the one Spirit to drink."[86]

You see, the church is—or should be—a place where each individual, every person, is valued as a part of the whole. Paul says that just as the human body is a single unit made up of many individual parts, "so it is with Christ."

> Whether you are Jew or Greek,
> slave or free,
> right-handed or left-handed,
> blonde or brunette,
> male or female,
> short or tall,
> Democrat or Republican,
> Libertarian or Independent,
> married or single,
> whether you drink Diet Mountain Dew or
> that frou-frou Perrier water,
> there is a place for you in the Body of Christ.

A Unique Place

Paul continues talking about the body:

> Even so the body is not made up of one part but of many.

Now if the foot should say, "Because I am not a hand, I do not belong to the body," it would not for that reason stop being part of the body. And if the ear should say, "Because I am not an eye, I do not belong to the body," it would not for that reason stop being part of the body. If the whole body were an eye, where would the sense of hearing be? If the whole body were an ear, where would the sense of smell be? But in fact God has placed the parts in the body, every one of them, just as he wanted them to be. If they were all one part, where would the body be? As it is, there are many parts, but one body.[87]

God has arranged a place *for you* in the Body of Christ, in the family of God, that is unique to you. And it's a place that corresponds to your spiritual gifts *and* to the needs of your church and community.

When the Jerusalem church faced the problem of food not getting distributed to all the widows in their care, they did not call for volunteers. They identified seven individuals whose God-given gifts (primarily wisdom and trustworthiness) recommended them for the task. The existence of the need was evidence that the correspondingly gifted people were already in the church, waiting to be found.

You may not yet know what your gift is—or, then again, maybe you do—but one thing's for sure: God does! He knows just how and where you fit in, because he's wisely and lovingly designed you and arranged for you to fulfill his design in a way that pleases him, fulfills you, and benefits every one of us. There is a unique place for you in the church that stretches all the way around the globe, from here to Mandalay and back again, and in your local church as well. And the presence of you and your gifts in that church indicates that God knows there is—or soon will be—a need your gifts will fill.

An Important Place

As Paul continues his long discussion of spiritual gifts and the way the church is supposed to function (in contrast to most "volunteer organizations" we see around us), he says this:

> The eye cannot say to the hand, "I don't need you!" And the head cannot say to the feet, "I don't need you!" On the contrary, those parts of the body that seem to be weaker are indispensable, and the parts that we think are less honorable we treat with special honor. And the parts that are unpresentable are treated with special modesty, while our presentable parts need no special treatment. But God has put the body together, giving greater honor to the parts that lacked it, so that there should be no division in the body, but that its parts should have equal concern for each other. If one part suffers, every part suffers with it; if one part is honored, every part rejoices with it.
>
> Now you are the body of Christ, and each one of you is a part of it.[88]

I don't know if you are an eye or a hand, a foot or a toe. You may not know, either. And for all *you* know, I could be a heel. But the point is: no matter what your spiritual gift is or isn't, you are nonetheless important, significant, "indispensable" (to use Paul's word), and worthy of honor.

Whether your gift is working with kids or computers, helping the poor or helping with worship, preaching or hospitality, leadership or mercy, every Christian, every gift, is crucial to the smooth and effective functioning of the church, the Body of Christ. This does not mean that none of us should clean a toilet or greet a visitor in the church unless we're gifted in those areas; all of us are called to serve. We must always remember that Jesus rebuked his first followers for considering some forms of service beneath them.[89] True servants will pitch in when and where they can. (For example, though my spiritual gifts are in the areas of preaching and teaching, I have been blessed as I mopped floors, cleaned kitty litter pans, and even shoveled raw sewage for the glory of God.) But wisdom—and the teaching of Scripture—should guide us to focus our best efforts on those areas where God has prepared us and placed us for effective service in the power of the Holy Spirit.

Every Part Plays a Part

Dizzy Dean was one of the greatest—and most colorful—baseball pitchers of all time. He once won thirty games in a season. He and his brother, who was nicknamed Daffy, each pitched two victories for the St. Louis Cardinals in the 1934 World Series, which St. Louis won, four games to three.

On one memorable day earlier that season, Dizzy Dean swaggered into the opposing team's locker room and told each hitter exactly how he would pitch to him, and then he went out and did exactly what he said, pitching a shutout and winning, 13 to 0.

But one day in 1937, Dizzy hurt his big toe—a minor injury, nothing important. After all, it was only a toe, right?

But it *was* important. He began favoring that toe, which affected his pitching motion, which affected his arm. And by the time he considered that toe to be important and took his injury seriously, his pitching arm was so severely affected that his career was over.

Because, you see, the pitching arm cannot say to the big toe, "You're not important; I don't need you." On the contrary, every person, every gift, is incredibly important. You are important, and the place God has arranged for you is an important place, and each of us needs what all the others have to offer.

∿ *Prayer*

Lord, drive home the realization that each person has important work in the kingdom of God. Show me how I fit into your plan for your kingdom, your church, your people, and your family. Open my eyes. Guide my steps. Help me to identify my gift and find my place—the place of fun, fulfillment, and fruitfulness for which you've designed me—and let me be diligent and wise in the service I offer, in Jesus' name. Amen.

CHAPTER SEVEN

Quit Being Nice

I used to sit next to Doug in choir.

I wasn't a pastor at the time; Doug and I attended the same nonde-
nominational church. Every week as choir rehearsal was beginning, Doug
would sit down next to me and ask, "Did you see *The Simpsons* last night?"

I had not.

Every week, I told him I had not. And every week, he would regale me
with what he considered the funniest highlights of the previous night's
episode. This happened week after week, until I finally decided (when
my two children were nowhere in the vicinity) to check out an episode. I
quickly decided that Doug's "highlight reel" was much funnier than the
show itself. So I continued to depend on his weekly relay of the funniest
bits from the show.

Doug's favorite *Simpsons* character was Ned Flanders, the next-door
neighbor of Homer and Marge Simpson and their children. Ned is an

evangelical Christian. Ned's doorbell chimes "A Mighty Fortress Is Our God." He leads his family in prayers at mealtimes and bedtimes. He attends church several times a week. He lives his life by the "three C's": "clean living, chewing thoroughly, and a daily dose of 'vitamin church.'" He endures regular abuse from the Simpsons, prompting Homer to claim in one episode that "this man has turned every cheek on his body."

Ned's manner of speaking is syrupy sweet and always cheerful. He eschews the normal "Hello" or "Good morning" for greetings like "Howdily-doo," "Howdily-doodily-do," and "Heidily-ho, neighbors." Others may say "yes" or "okay," but not Ned. He prefers, "Okily-dokily" and "Indeedily-doodily." And when he leaves, he may say "Toodily-doo" as he goes "skidaddly-doo."

It's all a bit much. A caricature. He *is* a cartoon character, after all. But behind the exaggeration hides a truth that makes Ned Flanders both familiar and funny. And it's this: Christians are nice.

Pleasantville People

Pleasantville was a 1998 movie about a place that remained stuck in the appearance, styles, and morals of a 1950s sitcom. It was neat and clean. Quaint and polite. Innocent and orderly. In a word, Pleasantville was "swell."

Ned Flanders would be right at home in Pleasantville. And so would most Christians and church folk. Many of us have been conditioned from the cradle to be pleasant, proper, and polite. We may not literally curtsey and bow to people we meet, but that's the general idea. We turn the other cheek—even, like Ned Flanders, every cheek on our bodies. We learn to cooperate. To conform.

To be nice.

We may never quite put it in so many words, but nearly all Christians share the "nice" gene. We want people to like us. We're "Christians," and that means we're not mean, rude, obstreperous, or cantankerous. We don't insult people. We don't offend people. We strive at all times for our lifestyle and personality to be charming and winsome, so as to attract people to the gospel of Jesus Christ.

I grew up in a loving Christian family. In many ways, my childhood was little different than that of Opie on the *Andy Griffith Show*—except that I had a father and mother, two older brothers, and no Aunt Bea. But otherwise, Opie's upbringing and mine seemed similarly idyllic. Except that on Sundays, once my family all got home from church, I was not allowed to play in the front yard. Only on Sundays. I don't know if I ever questioned the rule, but I had a vague understanding that it was simply not proper to play in the front yard on Sundays. The back yard, sure. And Monday through Saturday, the front yard was open for business. But not on Sundays.

Playing cards ("the devil's cards") were also frowned upon in our home, though we were all avid game-players. Gamblers used such things. We did not. No one said it would be sinful to play a heated hand of Hearts. But gamblers were not nice people, and we were.

The prohibition even extended to dice in my grandfather's home. He lived in Missouri. His favorite game—he played it every chance he got— was Trouble, a game with a Pop-O-Matic die in the center of the game board. The Pop-O-Matic device was a single, six-sided die inside a clear plastic bubble. Instead of rolling the die on the table (as in Monopoly and other games), players simply pressed the plastic bubble, causing the die to pop around inside its clear cage. It was quite an innovation in game technology.

We played Trouble for hours whenever we visited Grandpa—or he visited us—and yet we never once used the Pop-O-Matic die. Instead, we passed around the table a little arrow on a cardboard spinner, which we spun to determine our next move. The die remained untouched in its protective Pop-O-Matic housing. Because dice were tainted. Dice were used by gamblers. It probably wasn't a sin to "pop" one little die for our harmless game of Trouble, but it just wouldn't have been right somehow. You've got to have principles.

The "nice" ethic extended beyond the games we played. One of the most memorable moments of my childhood was one day when I came into the house from playing—I think by myself. I must have had an extensive track record of getting unspeakably dirty when I played, with others or by myself. The diabolical nature of this particular trait was amplified by the fact that my most frequent playmate in those years was a slightly older, similarly redheaded kid named Chip. Chip was not like me. He never got dirty. Somehow, we could crawl around under the porch or in elevator shafts (that's an entirely different story), and he would come out fresh as a rosebud after a rainstorm. I, on the other hand, would be indistinguishable from Charlie Brown's friend Pig-Pen.

On this particular occasion, I arrived in the kitchen. Where my mother greeted me. With something akin to horror. I don't recall if she marched me to the tub or hosed me down outside. I just remember her words: "Why can't you be more like Chip? He never gets dirty."

To this day, I don't know the answer to that question. And I'm sure my mom didn't mean to hurt my feelings. She'd probably had a rough day or a long week. But the message was clear. I should be neater. Cleaner. Nicer.

Unfortunately, I haven't improved much over the years. Ask my wife. But those rules—and others like them—sent messages that combined in my young, impressionable brain to create a high value for "nice" behaviors. Neat. Safe. Inoffensive.

Like Jesus.

Gentle Jesus, Meek and Mild

Our concept of Christian niceness derives in part from our images of a nice Christ. In much of our preaching, teaching, writing, and reading of recent generations, we have painted a distorted picture of Jesus. Author Paul Coughlin writes:

> Many of us believe in a wooden Jesus who was perpetually somber, consistently robotic, consummately nice. He wouldn't *think* of hurling sarcasm at anyone; his momma raised a Nice Boy with impeccable manners. Many sermons we hear are designed to make Jesus appear *always* approachable, *always* calm, and *endlessly* patient. That's fiction right up there with *The Da Vinci Code*; this mild Jesus has more to do with Eastern mysticism than with the Gospel record. He did *not* remain "above it all," emotionally hovering above us silly little humans. He got down in the muck and mire of life with us. . . .
>
> Looking back, I once believed this caricature of "gentle Jesus, meek and mild" because it was what I internalized during well-orchestrated church services designed to make God palatable to contemporary taste buds. I was told, though not in so many words, that the safe and pleasant route is really the best.[90]

I was, too. Again, not in so many words. But I grew up and entered ministry—and continued in ministry for many years—with a general belief that Christians were supposed to be nice. It was engrained. It was largely unquestioned.

No more.

Disturbing the Peace

Jesus, the teacher from Nazareth, the miracle-worker from Galilee, the rabbi everyone seemed to be talking about, entered the Holy City of Jerusalem that day riding a young donkey amid a raucous crowd that waved palm branches, sang his praises, and hailed him as the Son of David, their deliverer.

It was a bold thing to do, a clear, electrifying, symbolic act by which Jesus identified himself with the one spoken of by the prophet:

> Rejoice greatly, Daughter Zion!
>   Shout, Daughter Jerusalem!
> See, your king comes to you,
>   righteous and victorious,
> lowly and riding on a donkey,
>   on a colt, the foal of a donkey.[91]

The crowd understood what was happening. They followed Jesus and his disciples all the way to the temple precincts, where Jesus stood, tall and erect, and silently surveyed the scene. Moneychangers clattered their coins, taking advantage of travelers to the temple who had to exchange their foreign currencies for temple coins; cattle merchants yelled to attract the attention of those who had come to make their sacrifices, while the animals stamped and bellowed in fear; worshippers of all colors and tongues helplessly tried to bargain with the hucksters, whose bribes and under-the-table agreements enabled them to charge outlandish prices. And all of this in the temple of God, the place of his presence, the holy dwelling place of the Most High.

For a tense moment, Jesus stood rooted to the spot. And then, still watching, he snatched up strands of rope that had been dropped by one of the cattle herders. He began to turn them and tie them like a sailor, until suddenly, with a fury that seemed to crackle from his eyes, he started forward and snapped the knotted cord in his hands like a whip.

Even before his nicked and knotted carpenter's body reached the money tables, those who had seen him stalk their way hurriedly started from their seats and from the anger that blazed in his eyes. With every move he made, the scourge in his hand thrashed like something alive. With athletic economy and fluidity of movement, he drove the sheep and oxen out of the courts. Doves flew high over the temple walls, released from shattered cages. Jesus reached the tables of the greedy bankers and merchants and overturned them, scattering coins and weights in all directions. Some men clung to their tables or tried to retrieve their wares. Some ran after their cattle, while others cowered in corners or made a hasty exit from the violent noise and confusion.

By the time he stopped amid all the broken cages, overturned tables, and slack-jawed onlookers, everyone there knew what had just happened. They looked on the scene with astonishment and recalled the words of David, the poet-king: "Zeal for your house consumes me."[92]

No More Namby-Pamby

Most of us are accustomed to pictures of Jesus that portray him softly, with airbrushed cheeks and glistening hair. His hands are smooth, his eyes serene, his expression sweet. Above all, he is nice. Unfailingly. Unstintingly. Nice.

But I agree with the preacher Peter Marshall, who said, "We have had enough of the emaciated Christ, the pale, anemic, namby-pamby Jesus, the 'gentle Jesus meek and mild.' Perhaps we have had too much of it. Let us see the Christ of the gospels, striding up and down the dusty miles of Palestine, sun-tanned, bronzed, fearless."[93]

He's right. That is the Christ of the Gospels. The real Jesus of history.

Do you suppose his hands were soft? That *he* is soft?

He Is Not Soft

Some scholars think the "cleansing of the temple," which I described above, happened once, on Palm Sunday, as very similar incidents are described in all four New Testament Gospels. Others think Jesus did this more than once, early in his ministry (as John described in John 2), and later, on Palm Sunday, just days before his dying Passion.

In any case, it is John who tells us that Jesus "made a whip out of cords and drove all from the temple courts."[94] Does that sound like "gentle Jesus, meek and mild"? Does that bear any resemblance to the haloed portraits in some churches? Does it present a "nice" picture of Jesus?

Jesus with a whip?

Jesus wielding a weapon?

Was it just stagecraft, or did he intend to use it somehow?

Do you think he used it on people? On animals?

Do you think the time he took to make the whip demonstrates calm, not rage?

Know what I think?

I think he made a whip because he is not soft. He is serious about sin. About oppression. About extortion. About injustice. Even when it wears the robes of religiosity.

I don't think he used the whip to hurt anyone or any creature. But I think he used it to warn everyone that he was *not playin'*.

He Is Not Safe

C. S. Lewis wrote a scene in his story *The Lion, the Witch, and the Wardrobe* in which Mr. Beaver mentioned Aslan, and Susan asked, "Who is Aslan?"

"Why, don't you know?" [said Mr. Beaver.] "He's the King. He's the Lord of the whole wood. . . . He is in Narnia at this moment. He'll settle the White Queen all right."

And then Susan said:

"Is he—quite safe? I shall feel rather nervous about meeting a lion."

"That you will, dearie, and make no mistake," said Mrs. Beaver; "if there's anyone who can appear before Aslan without their knees knocking, they're either braver than most or else just silly."

"Then he isn't safe?" said Lucy.

"Safe?" said Mr. Beaver; "don't you hear what Mrs. Beaver tells you? Who said anything about safe? 'Course he isn't safe. But he's good."[95]

That depiction is one of C. S. Lewis's most often-quoted passages, and deservedly so, because it is true. Jesus is the Lion of Judah, the Alpha and Omega, the Mighty God, the Lord, mighty in battle, mighty in deed and word, the Rock of Ages, a Stone, the Living Stone, a Tried Stone, the Chief Cornerstone, a Stone of Stumbling, and a Rock of Offense. He's faithful and true, King of Kings, Lord of Lords, the One that John, the Gospel writer, would describe as:

Faithful and True. With justice he judges and wages war. His eyes are like blazing fire, and on his head are many crowns. He has a name written on him that no one knows but he himself. He is dressed in a robe dipped in blood, and his name is the Word of God. The armies of heaven were following him, riding on white horses and dressed in fine linen, white and clean. Coming out of his mouth is a sharp sword with which to strike down the nations. "He will rule them with an iron scepter." He treads the winepress of the fury of the wrath of God Almighty. On his robe and on his thigh he has this name written:

KING OF KINGS AND LORD OF LORDS.[96]

Does that sound safe to you? Nice?

Does that sound like someone you can put in a box? Keep for future reference? Call on when you feel like it?

No.

He is good. He is loving. He is gracious. But he is not safe.

He is not to be trifled with. He holds a whip. He is dressed in a robe dipped in blood. And from his mouth comes a sharp sword. He will be taken seriously.

He Is Not Satisfied

John records how, when Jesus had stormed through the temple courts like a tornado, upturning tables, driving out merchants, and frightening countless animals and birds, "His disciples remembered that it is written: 'Zeal for your house will consume me.'"[97]

Zeal for your house consumes me.

Do you know what his house is today?

Not the temple. It was destroyed in 70 AD and has not yet been rebuilt.

Not the church building where you worship.

Do you know what his house is today?

You.

The Bible says, "Do you not know that your body is a temple of the Holy Spirit?"[98]

The same zeal Jesus had for his house that first Palm Sunday, he has for his house today. Why would you expect otherwise?

He zealously cleaned his temple that day long ago. Is he less zealous today? Is he less concerned with the things that mar his house today? Are his standards lower now?

I don't think so. And I think it grieves him to see his followers worshipping some pale image of himself instead of the true and living Christ. I think it hurts him deeply that we esteem "niceness"—which he never taught—above Christlikeness. I believe Jesus calls us to conform to his image, not to our pseudo-Christian portraits of him. He does not call us to be nice.

He calls us to be real.

Getting Real

The problem, as Julius Caesar told Brutus, is "not in our stars, but in ourselves."[99] We like popularity more than principle. We have settled for blandness instead of boldness. We act as if Jesus changed our hearts—and removed our backbones.

That is why, to many people, Christians just aren't real. They're inauthentic. Fakey-fakey.

We even use terms like *fakey-fakey*.

And if we really take an honest look at ourselves, we would have to say they're right. We do wear masks. We do keep up appearances. We do find it hard to truly let other people—even other churchgoing people—see who we really are.

And that's a problem. *The Message* paraphrase says in Romans 12:9: "Love from the center of who you are. Don't fake it."

That is authenticity. Loving from what you're really like inside, acting from the center of who you are, not faking it. What you see is what you get. You don't pretend to be something you're not. You don't play a role. No charades. No facade. No mask.

Real.

It is not something most of us are accustomed to. But it is something we are called to be. Commanded to be. But how? Is it even possible for a person who has spent a lifetime being "nice" to learn to be real?

It is. It may not be easy, but it is possible, and it is well worth it. Not just at the destination (which I haven't reached yet) but all along the journey.

꠸ꠥ   ꠸ꠥ   ꠸ꠥ

The Velveteen Rabbit is a children's story that has delighted generations since its publication in 1922. It tells the story of a stuffed rabbit and his longing to be real. When the Rabbit is given to a boy one Christmas, he meets the Skin Horse, another toy in the household.

> "What is REAL?" asked the Rabbit one day, when they were lying side by side near the nursery fender, before Nana came to tidy the room. "Does it mean having things that buzz inside you and a stick-out handle?"
>
> "Real isn't how you are made," said the Skin Horse. "It's a thing that happens to you. When a child loves you for a long, long time, not just to play with, but REALLY loves you, then you become Real."
>
> "Does it hurt?" asked the Rabbit.
>
> "Sometimes," said the Skin Horse, for he was always truthful. "When you are Real you don't mind being hurt."

"Does it happen all at once, like being wound up," he asked, "or bit by bit?"

"It doesn't happen all at once," said the Skin Horse. "You become. It takes a long time."[100]

As the Skin Horse says, becoming real doesn't happen all at once. It is a process. But a few key adjustments in our *modus operandi* can pave the way for the authentic lives we are called to.

Supplant Your Fears

When God put Adam and Eve on the earth and they blew it and sin entered the world, fear also entered the world. Genesis 3 tells of how God spoke to Adam after his sin, and Adam admitted to a major relationship problem with God. He said, "I was afraid . . . so I hid."[101]

And we've been hiding ever since.

That is the main reason we are so "nice." We are afraid. Of all kinds of things.

We fear exposure. We try to be "nice" so people won't find us out, won't uncover who we *really* are. We don't mind our strengths being exposed. We don't mind our capabilities being exposed. We don't mind all the good things about us being exposed. But we don't want people to learn our weaknesses, our insecurities, our inadequacies. We don't want people to know that we don't have it all together. So we pretend, never letting anyone close enough to see the real "me."

We fear rejection. Many years ago, John Powell wrote a well-known book called *Why Am I Afraid to Tell You Who I Am?* The book runs to more than 150 pages. But it shouldn't take that many pages to answer the question. The answer is simple: I'm afraid to tell you who I am and what I'm really like because you might not like me. *And I'm all I've got.* But that kind of fear doesn't really protect you, it disables you. Proverbs 29:25 in *The Message* says, "The fear of human opinion disables."

It does. The fear of human opinion pressures me to be "nice" instead of being real. It forces me to try to be somebody else instead of myself. It prevents me from letting people know who I am, what I really think, and how I truly feel.

We fear being overlooked. We are addicted to the approval of other people. We want to be noticed. We want others to think highly of us. And—whether consciously or subconsciously—we reason that others will approve of us if we are nice, but not if we are real. Paul Coughlin says, "I have a non-Christian friend who says he can spot Christians at Hollywood parties: 'They worship at the altar of other people's approval.'"[102]

These fears are very real. They are controlling. They cannot simply be shrugged off. They can only be supplanted.

Many studies have shown that your self-esteem—how you feel about yourself—is largely determined by what you think the most important person in your life thinks about you. So let me suggest something very simple: make sure Jesus Christ is the most important person in your life. Because his love for you is unconditional, unmerited, unstoppable, and unfathomable. He knows you completely. He understands you. He values you. And he proved it by dying on a cross.

When you have that kind of love in your life, you can be free. When you meditate on that love and bask in it, you will be set free to be authentic. The more you realize how much Jesus Christ loves you and the more you feel it—not in your head but in your whole body, in your soul, in your gut—the freer you're going to be to drop the mask, quit pretending, quit faking it, and start becoming real. That's exactly what the Bible means when it says, "Perfect love drives out fear."[103]

So supplant your fears with the love of Jesus Christ for you. Whatever it takes, however you install that "data chip" into your heart and mind, let his love cast out those fears and set you free to be real.

Strive for Accountability

You probably know the story of King David in the Bible. You are probably also familiar with the time he lost his way spiritually and morally, how he lusted and compromised and committed adultery with Bathsheba and had her husband Uriah murdered to cover it all up. And you may recall how Nathan the prophet appeared and told him a homely little story about a rich man who stole a poor man's lamb—and he used that story to expose David's sin.

But have you ever stopped to ask, "How did Nathan get into the palace?" "How did he gain access to the court?" "How did he have the guts to say to the king, 'You are the man?'"

The answer is: he had been granted that access long before.

2 Samuel 7 tells how David bounced ideas off Nathan, got his counsel about building a temple for God, and made himself accountable to the prophet. So by the time the whole sordid affair with Bathsheba began, David had a friend in his life who had the authority to speak truth, to speak bluntly, to advise, *and* to correct him.

Everyone needs that. Every follower of Jesus needs a Nathan in his or her life. An accountability partner, as Nathan was to David, as Jethro was to Moses, as Barnabas was to Paul—somebody who loves you but is not impressed by you, not fooled by you. Someone you can trust, someone who will love you no matter what, someone to whom you can confess your fears, doubts, and sins,[104] and someone to whom you can be accountable. Someone with whom you can be real and to whom you've given the authority to challenge you and, when necessary, correct you.

This kind of relationship is absolutely crucial on the journey of becoming real. I have relied on accountability relationships for many years. They help me to be real, not only in our weekly meetings, but outside those meetings and with others as well. I always know there is at least one person in my circle of friends who knows the absolute worst about me and loves me anyway. That fact gives me the courage to be more authentic with others.

As the Skin Horse said, it doesn't happen all at once. It takes time to develop the honesty and transparency you'll need. I've actually approached friends in the past with a suggestion we just have lunch together every week for a while, and during that time I've just been testing the water, measuring whether we might reach a point of mutual accountability. With some, it was apparent early on that though we were good friends, we would not reach the level of trust and transparency necessary for mutual accountability. At other times, the relationship deepened fairly quickly. But every one has contributed, helping me become more real and more like the standard Paul sets in 2 Corinthians 4:2 (*The Message*): "We refuse to wear masks and play games. . . . Rather, we keep everything we do and say out in the open, the whole truth on display, so that those who want to can see."

As Edgar says in the final lines of Shakespeare's *King Lear*, we must "Speak what we feel, not what we ought to say."[105] We must live that way, too. That is authenticity. It is what you and I are called to. And it will get the world's attention.

Stop Stuffing Your Feelings

My friend and longtime co-pastor John Johnson once told his church:

> Nice is a defense mechanism; it's not something we do for others, but something we do for ourselves. It took me a long

time to figure this out, but I finally got it. Here's how: I can remember when I was a kid, my mom saying, "Play nice with your little brother." Of course, a voice deep inside me said, "Big brothers aren't supposed to play nice with their kid brothers; you're supposed to be hard, cruel, and antagonistic." I finally realized when I had more than one child in my own home that Mom didn't want me to play nice with my little brother for *his* sake, or for mine. She needed the peace! Nothing wrong with that, and I totally understand now.[106]

Many of us grew up learning how to "play nice." That's a valuable message. But a corollary to that law usually runs as deep: "Don't let your negative feelings show." And, to be fair, one of the necessary lessons of childhood is to show respect to parents and others. But often our behavior goes beyond respect to an expectation that we should be "nice" even when we feel anger, hurt, indignation, and so on.

But that is not the way of Jesus. He tells us if we have something against a brother (or a brother has something against us), to say something, rather than stuffing our feelings.[107] The Bible actually says we should "be angry and do not sin."[108] It is possible—and utterly Christlike—to display the full range of human emotions, from joy to despair, without sinning. In fact, sometimes it is sinful to ignore or suppress our emotions, as radio talk show host Paul Coughlin points out in his book, *No More Christian Nice Guy*:

> Dan, an infrequent radio caller of mine, expressed the prevalent view among evangelical men and how squeamish they are when it comes to the necessity of physical defense. When we devoted a show to whether or not a kid should stand up to a schoolyard bully, Dan called to say he believes only in "fighting

with prayer." He said he's taught all his children that if someone humiliates them, the humiliation is good for them, part of God's will—they should suffer for righteousness' sake.

My co-host, Bill Gallagher, says I nearly turned purple.

"Dan," I replied, "most kids aren't being picked on at school for righteousness' sake. They're being picked on because they wear glasses, are ugly, pretty, tall, short, because their hairstyle is six months behind the fashion curve."

So let's take off the spiritual veneer. "Dan," I went on, "what would you do if your prayers went unanswered and your daughter was still being picked on by a mean boy at school?"

Dan, like so many evangelical men, actually said he'd let the humiliation continue. In some misguided notion of meekness and humility, he would allow his daughter to be beaten both physically and emotionally by a person who should be detained somewhere. This still makes me angry. She wouldn't be suffering for the Lord, she'd be suffering because her father's a Christian Nice Guy, a man so fearful of conflict that he hides behind a distorted misrepresentation of God to give his fear a spiritual glimmer. Imagine the abandonment his daughter would experience, the pathetic outlook she would form about men, about her father, about her Father.[109]

So stop stuffing your feelings. Let God (and others) help you express your emotions—even anger—without sinning.

Start Saying No

Many of us struggle with impossible schedules, unrealistic expectations, and stressful lives because we can't say no. Someone asks us to volunteer for something at church, and we can't turn him down. Another person approaches us to help with a bake sale, and we agree. Still others beg us to help relieve some of the pressure *they* are under, and we comply. We may already be overbooked. We may be stressed. We may be neglecting other, more important responsibilities. But we can't say no. It wouldn't be nice.

Jesus said, "Don't say anything you don't mean. . . . Just say 'yes' and 'no.'"[110] He himself said no at times. When his followers pressured him not to visit a sick friend in a dangerous area, he said no.[111] When his friends thought he should return to a nearby town to heal the throngs of people who were looking for him, he said no.[112] When his friend Martha urged him to put her sister Mary in her place, he said no.[113]

Followers of Jesus are not obligated to say yes to every demand or expectation. *He* didn't. We shouldn't.

Dr. Henry Cloud and Dr. John Townsend, in their important book, *Boundaries*, say:

> The most basic boundary-setting word is *no*. It lets others know that you exist apart from them and that you are in control of you. Being clear about your no—and your yes—is a theme that runs throughout the Bible (Matt. 5:37; James 5:12).
>
> *No* is a confrontational word. The Bible says that we are to confront people we love, saying, "No, that behavior is not okay. I will not participate in that." The word *no* is also important in setting limits on abuse. Many passages of Scripture urge us to say no to others' sinful treatment of us (Matt. 18:15-20).[114]

As Charles Haddon Spurgeon—the Prince of Preachers—famously said, "Learn to say 'no.' It will be of more use to you than to be able to read Latin."

The Skin Horse was right: "Being real isn't how you are made." But it can happen to you. It is what you are called to, if you are a follower of Jesus Christ, the ultimate Reality. It can hurt. But when you are real, the hurt is worth it. If we can by God's grace find the courage to overcome our fears, if we can refuse to wear masks and stop playing games, if we can put the whole truth on display so that those who want to can see the reality of a life that is lived in the light—*wow*! Can you see how that will affect the people around us, what a testimony it will be for the people who are watching?

So quit being "nice." Love from the center of who you are, as Jesus did.

Prayer

Dear God, I want to quit being nice. I don't want to pretend to be something I'm not, or to feel something I don't. I don't want to play a role. No charades. No facade. No mask. I want to be honest about who I am, and even honest about the progress I have yet to make. I want to learn to be real. I want to go through life loving others from the center of who I am, not faking it.

You know my fears. You know my hesitations. You know my need. Please help me to live in the light of your love. Help me to become a more open, loving, and authentic person, as I make you Lord of my life, day by day. Amen.

CHAPTER EIGHT

Quit Helping the Poor

I grew up in the Salvation Army.

You know, the bell ringers and red kettles at Christmastime. The "soup, soap, and salvation" people. Thrift stores and uniforms and brass bands.

A lot of people don't know that the Salvation Army is not only a charitable organization operating in well over a hundred countries around the world; it is also a Christian denomination, a church with ministers (officers) and members (soldiers) who worship in more than 175 languages.

During my growing-up years in Cincinnati, Ohio, I wasn't particularly anxious to admit that my family worshipped at the Salvation Army. When my suburban classmates asked where I went to church, I would respond, "Downtown." If they pressed the question, I would say, "On Central Parkway." When I could no longer escape the inevitable, I would tell them it was the Salvation Army and brace myself for the predictable barrage of laughter and ridicule.

Someone would compliment the jacket or shirt I was wearing: "I used to have one just like it," he would say. "But then my mom gave it to the Salvation Army"—suggesting, of course, that that's where mine came from. Very funny. The worst thing about that joke (and many others like it) was that I fell for it every time. Oh, and also that it might have been true.

But over the years, my embarrassment about calling the Salvation Army my church lessened, and my pride—a healthy pride, I think—grew. Even before starting first grade, I had worshipped hundreds of times in one of the worst urban areas of Cincinnati, where my parents led a satellite Sunday school that the Salvation Army had planted in the projects. I think I recognized that those children lived in different circumstances than I did, but I don't recall ever thinking of them as "poor." They were just kids.

Starting when I was nine years old, my church hosted a Sunday morning breakfast for the Over-the-Rhine neighborhood in Cincinnati, and it seemed like my family was always in attendance (probably because my mom was a gifted pianist, and my dad led singing and delivered a short Bible message much of the time). I met some of the most memorable people of my life at those Sunday morning breakfasts. I didn't know that many of them were "street people," maybe because I knew most of them by name. I especially remember Fifi, who everyone said had once been a successful lawyer and was still rich, although you'd never know by looking at her. She waltzed into the Salvation Army breakfast area like a perennial prom queen, sometimes with a small dog in tow. And sometimes the dog sported a wig that matched whatever hairpiece Fifi wore. I recall one summer in particular when she safety-pinned dollar bills to her gauzy outfit and could be seen coming to and from our church with a train of men literally grasping and panting after her, trying to relieve her of some of her accoutrements. On another occasion, she gave the pastor, Major Bill Bender, a donation check . . . with the signature line blank. She proceeded to place the check in her mouth and leave a lipstick print on the signature line, front and back. The bank cashed it. (Major Bender even received a vote in a Cincinnati mayoral election; Fifi wrote in his name on the ballot.)[115]

As a young teenager, I spent many weekday nights and Sunday evenings accompanying my parents to Harbor Light services, where homeless and addicted men and women would worship and enjoy a hot meal and a warm bed for the night. At various times in my life, I probably had more alcoholic friends than otherwise.

On my sixteenth birthday, a series of deadly tornadoes (the largest tornado outbreak in history at the time) tore through Cincinnati and other southern Ohio towns. I spent the following week working with my father to take clothes, blankets, food, and water to people in those devastated areas. (He must have allowed me to stay out of school that week, which probably made me especially grateful for my church's orientation toward helping people.)

Late one night a week before my wedding, my fiancée and I had just walked in the door of her home when the phone rang. The Beverly Hills Supper Club, a popular nightclub just across the river from Cincinnati, had caught fire earlier that evening, and the attempted evacuation had become deadly. With many other Salvation Army volunteers, my fiancée and I worked through the night while the structure still smoldered and victims were still being carried out. While firefighters and other emergency personnel labored tirelessly, we carried water and other supplies back and forth to them. The next day, we assisted the pastoral counseling efforts taking place in the makeshift morgue at the nearby Ft. Thomas Armory.

Just eight months later, my new wife and I were living in Findlay, Ohio, next door to the Salvation Army church there, when the blizzard of 1978 hit the Ohio Valley and Great Lakes. (It's okay if you're starting to think these experiences had more to do with me being some sort of "disaster magnet" than with my involvement in the Salvation Army; I've often harbored the same suspicions.) Our church opened its doors to scores of stranded travelers and area residents who had lost power or couldn't get home. We cooked, cleaned, counseled, prayed, and entertained children for a week or more, simply grateful that our lives would someday return to "normal," while the lives of others (fifty-one people died as a result of the storm) wouldn't.

So I mean what I say: I got over my embarrassment at being a "Salvationist," as members of the Salvation Army call themselves. I suppose I've ladled thousands of bowls of soup, handed out thousands of blankets, distributed thousands of shoes and coats, provided thousands of toys to children, and helped thousands of kids attend a week at summer camp. I'm far from alone in those experiences, especially among my Salvationist friends. Any one of them could make similar claims.

Yet, in spite of that rich and rewarding background, I think it's time to face facts and urge you to quit helping the poor. Not that I don't think it's a path to great blessings, for you and for those you help. It is all that. But I don't believe helping the poor is particularly Christlike. It is not what Jesus modeled. Nor do I believe it is his will for your life.

Quit Helping the Poor

There's a story in the Gospels that has always bothered me. Actually, that's not quite accurate. It's not the story itself. It's what Jesus says in the story. But it is found in Matthew, Mark, and John, and all three Gospels report Jesus' words in pretty much the same way.

It happened just days before the momentous events of the Lord's Passion, those hours in which he was arrested, tried, tortured, and crucified. It took place in the home of Simon the Leper, and here is how it is recorded in John's Gospel:

> Six days before the Passover, Jesus came to Bethany, where Lazarus lived, whom Jesus had raised from the dead. Here a dinner was given in Jesus' honor. Martha served, while Lazarus was among those reclining at the table with him. Then Mary took about a pint of pure nard, an expensive perfume; she poured it on Jesus' feet and wiped his feet with her hair. And the house was filled with the fragrance of the perfume.
>
> But one of his disciples, Judas Iscariot, who was later to betray him, objected, "Why wasn't this perfume sold and the money given to the poor? It was worth a year's wages." He did not say this because he cared about the poor but because he was a thief; as keeper of the money bag, he used to help himself to what was put into it.
>
> "Leave her alone," Jesus replied. "It was intended that she should save this perfume for the day of my burial. You will always have the poor among you, but you will not always have me."[116]

I must admit, I have several problems with Jesus' response to Judas. I am not a fan of extravagance, for one. Perhaps due to my upbringing, I am a committed member of the "use it up, wear it out, make it do, or do without" school of economics. I experience physical pain when my wife cleans out the refrigerator and throws away old and expired containers of food. ("If I had eaten that last night, it wouldn't have gone to waste.") I rejoice that my car has 150,000 miles on the odometer and that my boots are on their third set of soles, and there are rumors in my family that I sneak snacks—and even drinks—into movie theaters (my spokesman can neither confirm nor deny those rumors).

But the larger problem I have with Jesus' words is their apparent insensitivity to the needs of the poor. Sure, Judas was on the take, but it seems to me he had a good point, nonetheless. And I get that Jesus was defending the worshipful Mary, who had done a loving, generous thing. I get that. But Jesus' reply still sounds uncaring.

It's not, though. First, unlike you and me, everyone in that room would have recognized in Jesus' words a reference to the Torah. When he said, "You will always have the poor among you," he was quoting from the commands of God given in the law: "There are always going to be poor and needy people among you. So I command you: Always be generous, open purse and hands, give to your neighbors in trouble, your poor and hurting neighbors."[117]

In other words, in his response to Judas's objection, Jesus was not excusing or embracing hardheartedness or tight-fistedness toward the poor. He was doing exactly the opposite. He was reminding everyone who was listening that God's law required generosity toward the poor. But he was doing something else as well.

The Poor Woman and the Rabbi

Another story from the Bible has gotten under my skin at times. Both Mark and Luke record it in their Gospels. Here's how Mark tells it:

> Jesus sat down opposite the place where the offerings were put and watched the crowd putting their money into the temple treasury. Many rich people threw in large amounts. But a poor

widow came and put in two very small copper coins, worth only a fraction of a penny.

Calling his disciples to him, Jesus said, "I tell you the truth, this poor widow has put more into the treasury than all the others. They all gave out of their wealth; but she, out of her poverty, put in everything—all she had to live on."[118]

I think I can deal with this passage's depiction of Jesus as a little bit nosy. I can also get beyond the problem of Jesus noticing what people were putting into the offering box. In most churches today, his behavior would be far beyond the bounds of polite behavior. Most of us try not to let other people see what we're putting in the offering, and we do our best to avert our eyes so no one will suspect us of inspecting their generosity (or lack of it). So, the Lord's behavior can seem a little off-putting in this story. (Of course, he is the Lord of all, and so he not only sees the treasurer's reports but is also the presumed recipient of our tithes and offerings. I suppose in that light it's not all that *gauche*.)

But again, that's not what gets under my skin about this story. It's the fact that Jesus somehow knows that this woman "put in everything—all she had to live on." How did he know that? Was it a form of supernatural knowledge? Did he know it in the same way that he knew the Samaritan woman had five husbands?[119] It could be, but I don't think so.

Was it just a reasonable guess? The way you or I might see a man sleeping on a park bench and say, "That poor homeless man," whether we knew him to be homeless or not? It could be, but I don't think so.

I think Jesus knew that this woman "put in everything—all she had to live on" because he knew her. Not supernaturally, but quite naturally, as a neighbor or a friend, or perhaps just a passing acquaintance. Maybe he'd met her in the marketplace. Maybe they'd talked at the temple. Jesus was always doing that sort of thing, you know.[120]

But there's something else. Something that is missed by nearly every reader of this passage. Jesus commends this woman, sure. He points her out to his followers from across the room. But as far as we know, he watched her put in "everything—all she had to live on"—and didn't commission one of his disciples to track her down and make a donation. He fed five thousand but apparently let this woman go home penniless. Of course, the story just ends; it's possible that there's much more to the story than we are told by either Mark or Luke, who recorded it. But I don't think so, because I believe there is a crucial point, both in this incident and in Jesus' response to the woman's generosity in anointing him for his burial, that we routinely miss.

Jesus Never Lived in Suburbia

It's often difficult for us to connect with the whole truth and full impact of the Bible's rich narrative because our lives are quite different from those lives. We tend to transplant twenty-first-century images and ideas onto the biblical narrative and so short-circuit a full understanding and appreciation of its life-changing words.

For example, we might read of Jesus eating in someone's home (like that of Simon the Leper) and picture a dining room table much like our own, with plates and spoons and forks. Or we might read a parable about a friend knocking on a neighbor's door at midnight and waking the inhabitants, and picture the home's inhabitants in beds and bedrooms much like our own. But neither of those mental images is accurate.

Those projections may be harmless. Or they may prevent us from understanding what is truly going on and how our lives should be affected. I think that is the case in these stories I've related, and I think our preconceptions negatively affect how we "help" the poor, as individuals and as the church.

Jesus did not live in suburbia. He was not middle class. He did not "help" the poor. He was *one of them.*

He was homeless.[121] He had to fish out a miracle in order to pay his taxes.[122] He slept in the homes of friends.[123] He rode into Jerusalem on Palm Sunday on a loaned donkey.[124] He celebrated his final Passover in someone's guest room.[125] He was buried in a borrowed tomb.[126] When Mary anointed him with expensive, fragrant oil, he was a poor man on the way to his death. When Jesus pointed out the poor widow who gave her all, he was a poor man who would soon make a similarly total offering.

This is the great difference between the "Jesus way" and our way of "helping" the poor. Most of us, living in immeasurably more affluent circumstances than Jesus or any of his followers, are removed from the poor—even insulated from them—in ways the first Christians could not have imagined. When Jesus said, "You will always have the poor among you,"[127] he meant, "*among* you." Not "on your drive to the office." Not "under the highway overpass." Not "in shelters," or "in barrios," or in neighborhoods far from your community. He meant *among* you.

Many of us live day after day, week after week, even year after year without any poor "among" us. We write checks. We pay taxes. We support causes. Sometimes we even volunteer a few hours at a soup kitchen. We might spend a week on a mission trip to help those in need. But we return home. The poor are not "among" us. Generally speaking, we don't *know* them. Which is why I say, quit helping the poor . . . and unite with them instead.

What the World Needs

Jesus didn't merely feel sympathy for the poor; he was one of them. He didn't reach out to them; he knew them already. He knew their names. He knew their circumstances. He knew their needs. His life intertwined with theirs.

This is one of the great needs of our time. Many followers of Jesus live antiseptic lives, so far removed from economic hardship that our efforts to "help" are ineffectual and, sometimes, counterproductive. What the world needs—and I believe what Christ calls us to—is economic justice that springs from relational justice. In other words, if we are "among" the poor and they are "among" us, we will all be changed, and we will be conformed to the image of Christ more and more as a result.

Shane Claiborne, in his book *The Irresistible Revolution*, tells how God changed his life through radical identification with the poor. He says that being among the poor often resulted in a sense of separation—distance—from the church:

> One day we received a box of donations from one of the wealthy congregations near our college that will remain nameless. Written in marker on the cardboard box were the words, "For the homeless." Excited, I opened it up, only to find the entire box filled with microwave popcorn. My first instinct was to laugh. We barely had electricity, much less a microwave, and popcorn wasn't on the top of the needs list. My second instinct was to cry because of how far the church had become removed from the poor. Later that same week, another group of folks brought donations by St. Ed's—the mafia. With the media jumping on the story, the mafia came by and gave bikes to each of the kids, turkeys to each family, and thousands of dollars to the

organization. I thought to myself, I guess God can use the mafia, but I would like God to use the church.[128]

When Jesus—and the Bible—talk about helping the poor, it is with the assumption that the poor are "among" us, that we have not so completely separated ourselves from the human suffering and messiness of poverty that we don't know people's names . . . or their true needs. Christlike attitudes and efforts toward the poor rely upon wealthy (or stable) Christians rubbing shoulders with the poor, getting to know them, treating them as real people, and intertwining their lives, as Jesus did. A biblical attitude will not only bridge the economic gap between rich and poor, but it will bridge the social gaps, also. When this happens, not only will blessing flow to the poor, but it will abound to the relatively-rich, resulting in joy and celebration that will cause a skeptical, cynical world to sit up and take notice.

Peter Leithart, pastor of Trinity Reformed Church in Moscow, Idaho, and Senior Fellow of Theology and Literature at New St. Andrews College, wrote this:

> **Especially in Deuteronomy, generosity to the poor is coupled with festivity.** When Israelites bring the tithe (tenth) of their harvest to the Lord's house, they celebrate with meat and strong drink, but are exhorted to remember the Levites, who have no land of their own (Deuteronomy 14:27). Every third year, a portion of the tithe is given to the alien, orphan, and widow who "shall come and eat and be satisfied" (Deuteronomy 14:28-29). At the annual feasts of Pentecost and Booths, too, the celebrants welcome those with no resources of their own (Deuteronomy 16:10-11, 13-14). Again, the rights of both owners and non-owners are honored. Landowners rejoice in

their abundance, but the landless poor share the abundance. The successful are not pilloried or punished, but the Lord commands them to open their hearts and their tables to the unsuccessful.[129]

Not just their hearts. Not just their checkbooks. But their tables, too. Our modern lifestyles may make Christlike attitudes and actions toward the poor a little less intuitive, but it's not impossible. And emulating Christ's actions may open our lives to blessings we have never experienced and might not have thought possible.

The Cleaning Woman and the Ironing Lady

Growing up, I was keenly aware that my family was the poorest on the block in our middle-class neighborhood. We were far from poor by some standards (and certainly by Jesus' standards), but what mattered to me at that time were my neighborhood's standards. My friends sported the latest fashions; I wore my brothers' hand-me-downs. Other homes on the block boasted fine furnishings and color televisions; our carpets were threadbare and I was convinced our black-and-white television was old enough to have broadcast John Cameron Swayze reporting the invention of the wheel. Other families parked two cars in their garages; my father worked long hours to keep our 1957 Ford Fairlane running, and my mother rode the bus an hour each way to her job every day.

Yet for all our apparent poverty, we were the only family I knew that employed an ironing lady *and* a cleaning woman. In the days before permanent press, my father would take a basket of clothes (which Mom had pre-dampened and rolled up) to a woman named Mers every week. Mers was a widow, and everyone called her "Mers." She even referred to herself that way—never "Mrs. Mers," just "Mers." She was a longtime member of the urban church we attended, and she exerted tyrannical control over the church kitchen; no one else was permitted even to make coffee, either in her presence or in her absence. She once chased me and a friend out of the kitchen, waving a butcher knife at us and effecting an eerie impression of the farmer's wife in "Three Blind Mice." To this day, I don't know how much—if any—of her threatened violence was an act.

But every week, the same scene played itself out. We would drive far across town to Mers's tenement apartment, pick up the basket of ironing, and pay her for her work. Once home, Mom took out the clothing piece by piece and ironed it again.

"Why do you do that?" I or one of my brothers would ask.

"She missed a spot," Mom would say.

"But you do this all the time," we would say. "Why do we pay Mers to iron for us if you're just going to do it over?"

Mom would sometimes blush. She surely felt the implied reproach in our words. But she would shrug or smile and say, "Mers needs the money."

It was the same with Mrs. Grubb, our cleaning lady. Another widow living on a limited income, Mrs. Grubb came to our house every week. She was a cheerless woman who seemed to approach every cleaning task as though my brothers and I had created it solely to make her life miserable. She was wrong, of course; there were other reasons. We paid for it, though. Mrs. Grubb left behind a wake of streaked windows, sticky linoleum floors, and half-dusted surfaces every Thursday. Every Saturday, Mom would put me and my brothers to work correcting Mrs. Grubb's cleaning job.

"Why do you do that?" one of us would ask.

"I don't want people to think we live in a pig sty," she would answer.

"But we wouldn't have to clean so much if we didn't have a cleaning lady," we would say. "Why do you pay her to clean if you're just going to make us do it over a couple days later?"

Of course, we knew what the answer would be. "Mrs. Grubb needs the money."

I never understood that. My mom died when I was still a boy, and her relationship with Mers and Mrs. Grubb mystified me for years. Even as I matured into adulthood, I occasionally reflected on my mother's quizzical behavior with a wry smile and a shake of the head. I always suspected that there might have been more to her arrangements with Mers and Mrs. Grubb than I could understand at the time, but I never quite got it. Until one day when my son arrived home from school and saw Tim, a friend of mine, painting my home office.

"Why is he doing that?" my son asked when we were out of Tim's earshot.

I shrugged. "Because I asked him to."

"But you just painted the whole first floor last year, didn't you?"

The words were out of my mouth before I knew it. "He needs the money," I said.

In that moment, I heard not my own voice, but my mother's. I remembered how often she had used such words in reference to Mers and Mrs. Grubb, and the light suddenly dawned in my mind and heart. I realized then that my mother had taught me more than I had given her credit for. She had modeled how to "give to the needy [without letting] your left hand know what your right hand is doing."[130] She had shown me how to enter into the lives of those who are less affluent and find ways to make common cause with them.

Giving Up Our Antiseptic Lives

My friends Ray and Sandy Jackson recently accepted a new ministry position at a Salvation Army church in Harlem. With the position came a
comfortable suburban parsonage in a solidly middle-class neighborhood.
But the Jacksons had a different idea. They arranged the purchase and
rehab of a home just ten blocks from the church. Though the area is not
as quiet, safe, or affluent as others they have lived in, they wanted to live
among the people to whom God had sent them.

Ray says the decision was the product of many factors, including fer-
vent prayer. "Truth be known, we had gotten comfortable with our suburban commute [in a previous position]. It was quite easy to work in the city
and escape every night and weekends to a quiet, tree-lined neighborhood.
We would not have to keep the windows closed against bus fumes and
police sirens, and we wouldn't be lulled to sleep by the rumble of subway
trains underground. But Jesus did not 'phone in' the Good News. He
didn't preach the Gospel then retreat to heaven at night. He moved into
the neighborhood. So we have, too. We believe this is where God wants
us: walking the neighborhood every day, living its ups and downs, living
incarnationally, becoming part of our neighbors' lives. It isn't always easy
and the needs are overwhelming, but so are the blessings."

Rob Bell, in his book *Velvet Elvis*, writes:

> I was just talking to a woman named Michelle who decided
> to move into the roughest neighborhood in our city to try to
> help people get out of the cycle of poverty and despair. She was
> telling me about the kids she is tutoring and the families they
> come from and how great the needs are. Some other women
> in our church heard about Michelle and asked her for lists of
> what exactly the families in her neighborhood need. (One of the

families wrote on their list "heat".) They then circulated the lists until they found people who could meet every one of the needs. It's like an underground mom-mafia network. Michelle told me at last count they had helped 430 families, and they are making plans to expand their network.[131]

Maybe not all of us can do that. Maybe not all of us *should* do that, necessarily. But there is more than one way to give up our antiseptic lives and unite with those who are far less affluent than we are. The early history of the church records such a moment in the lives of Peter and John:

Peter and John went to the Temple one afternoon to take part in the three o'clock prayer service. As they approached the Temple, a man lame from birth was being carried in. Each day he was put beside the Temple gate, the one called the Beautiful Gate, so he could beg from the people going into the Temple. When he saw Peter and John about to enter, he asked them for some money.

Peter and John looked at him intently, and Peter said, "Look at us!" The lame man looked at them eagerly, expecting some money. But Peter said, "I don't have any silver or gold for you. But I'll give you what I have. In the name of Jesus Christ the Nazarene, get up and walk!"

Then Peter took the lame man by the right hand and helped him up. And as he did, the man's feet and ankles were instantly healed and strengthened. He jumped up, stood on his feet, and began to walk! Then, walking, leaping, and praising God, he went into the Temple with them.

All the people saw him walking and heard him praising God. When they realized he was the lame beggar they had seen so often at the Beautiful Gate, they were absolutely astounded!

They all rushed out in amazement to Solomon's Colonnade, where the man was holding tightly to Peter and John.[132]

Peter and John were on their way to church, so to speak. They had no money on them. But they gave what they could. Sure, it was miraculous, but I truly believe the effect of God's people who identify and unite with the poor will be miraculous, too.

I like what Michael Spencer said in his book, *Mere Churchianity*:

> I was interviewed on a radio show a few months ago, and the host was prodding me a bit, since I'm known as a critic of the institutional church. He asked me where to find a really good church. He was out of church and didn't want to go back. My answer to him was simple: Go to the poor. Go to the storefront church. Go where they have no money to spend on technology. Go where the hungry are next door and the addicted are on the sidewalk outside. Go there, and you'll find Jesus.[133]

Identifying and uniting with the poor may take us out of our comfort zones. It may be inconvenient. It may require us to go out of our way. It may interrupt our plans. But it will be worth it, for us and for others. And as it did in those early days of the church, it will change lives and astound a watching world.

Prayer

God, what can I do? How can I quit "helping the poor" and find ways to unite with them, instead?

Is there somewhere I should go?

Something I should do?

Someone I should contact?

Some new involvement?

Some new awareness?

Is there a person whose path you want me to cross?

A family you want me to get to know?

A neighborhood or community you have in mind?

Save me, Lord God, from sending microwave popcorn to the homeless. Help me to do what you did, in Christ, and "move into the neighborhood" in whatever ways you lead me to do. Give me the faith and courage to send myself instead of only my silver or gold, in the name of Jesus, who for my sake became poor that I through his poverty might become rich.[134] Amen.

CHAPTER NINE

Quit Fellowshipping

We church folk love to eat. We enjoy covered dish suppers, spaghetti dinners, pancake breakfasts, all-you-can-eat fish fries, beans-and-cornbread fundraisers. And we've been known to serve coffee and donuts at the slightest provocation. But hey, we're called to "the fellowship of the saints," right?

When my wife, the lovely Robin, and I were newlyweds, we worshipped and served at a small Salvation Army church in Findlay, Ohio, where I was working hard to become a failed art student. Two of the members of that church were an elderly couple, Fred and Opal.

Fred would frequently "get blessed" in the course of worship. A line in a hymn or something the preacher said would touch him and he would clap vigorously, throw both hands up in the air as if waiting for an angel to slap a couple high fives on him, and say "yes, yes, yes" or "glory, hallelujah!" He would do this over and over, sometimes long after the hymn ended or the preacher moved into his next point. Opal, on the other hand, suffered from a form of palsy that seemed to affect her in only one way: she would frequently shake her head back and forth as if she were telling someone no, over and over.

Fred and Opal would always sit together in the middle of the little hundred-seat Salvation Army chapel during worship services. That chapel is where I preached one of the first sermons of my life. I couldn't tell you what text I chose. I can't recall anything I said. All I remember of that occasion is Fred and Opal, side by side, responding to my meticulously crafted sermon—Fred, by saying "yes" and clapping and high-fiving invisible angels, and Opal seemingly disagreeing with everything I said. Looking back, those moments of "yes" from Fred and "no" from Opal were pretty good preparation for the thirty-plus years of preaching I've done since that day, and I frequently remember them both, fondly, as I observe a similar variety of response every time I speak.

I also think of Opal nearly every time I attend a covered dish or potluck supper at church.

Keep That Dish Covered

Friends have sometimes referred to my wife as "the sweetest woman on earth." She has earned that moniker, and not only because she tolerates me. She is unfailingly kind, generous, and loving to everyone in her life. Her mercy and compassion flow long after my supply is utterly exhausted—which makes her response to Opal one day at a church supper all the more hilarious, in my view.

Though she was only twenty years old at the time, Robin had wisdom far beyond her years—partly because her parents were pastors—and particularly when it came to covered dish suppers (in which each family or household in the church brought a slow cooker or covered dish of some kind to contribute to a shared meal). In fact, she would often volunteer in the kitchen on those days, so that she would know just which cooks had donated what dishes. This was important insider information to have, especially in a widely varied church family that included people of vastly different backgrounds and, er, habits.

On this occasion, I think Robin had urged me to go ahead and fix myself a plate rather than wait for her while she finished up a few things in the kitchen. So, by the time she started through the line, spooning various casseroles and other culinary concoctions onto her plate, I had preceded her and sat down at a nearby table. That's when Opal sidled up beside her.

Opal pointed to a bowl of beans on the table. "Those are my beans."

The lovely Robin smiled and said something in reply, but she didn't spoon any of Opal's beans onto her plate.

"You should have you some beans," Opal said.

Robin smiled again and said something like, "I don't think I'm in the mood for beans today."

Opal would not be denied. "Bob took some."

"Oh, I know," Robin answered, moving farther down the table. "He'll eat anything."

It was a rare moment. Opal moseyed off, and neither she nor Robin seemed to really catch what Robin had said. But I couldn't just let it go. I don't have nearly that much class . . . or grace. So, once I stopped choking with laughter, I recreated the conversation I had just heard for Robin. She was mortified, of course. But I was highly entertained.

I suppose since that day we've enjoyed hundreds of church suppers, barbecues, receptions, and coffees. I blame them all for my less-than-svelte physique. And I suggest we really should cut it out. Not just for the sake of my weight, but for other reasons, too. For better reasons. We should quit fellowshipping.

Rethinking What We Do

Many of the ways we "do church" these days have practical or cultural—rather than biblical—origins. For example, church bells began to be used in Europe in the Middle Ages. They would be rung to signal the time for prayer (or each hour of the day), thus serving as an early means of mass communication for villages or larger areas.

Pews didn't become standard in churches until around the fifteenth century, about the time of the Reformation, when the sermon became more of a focal point in Protestant Christian worship. In some churches, members purchased or rented their pews, which were often arranged as boxes to accommodate whole families (and practically as well as symbolically fencing out those who couldn't afford the pew fees).

Likewise pulpits. Until the Protestant Reformation, pulpits were generally set off to one side and usually elevated, while the altar—the setting for the Mass—occupied the central position at the front of the church (this is still true in Roman Catholic practice, of course). The Reformation's emphasis on the preaching of the Word as central to Christian worship moved the pulpit to the center, where it has remained in many Protestant churches.

Even the use of the cross as a symbol—a highly venerated emblem among modern Christians, whether Orthodox, Catholic, or Protestant—mostly dates from the fourth century, not from the earliest days of the church. Writing in the late second century, Clement of Alexandria listed the preferred Christian symbols as a dove, fish, ship, musical lyre, or ship's anchor.[135]

So it is with church suppers. Sort of. The way most of us "fellow-ship" today does not hearken back to the practices of the New Testament church. Church suppers and other church "fellowship" events are of a far more recent vintage. And they can profitably be discarded, in my opin-ion—particularly if we replace them with something better, something that more closely resembles the way of Jesus and his earliest followers.

The Party That Didn't Die

The party had been going on for days, and all had gone well.

Jesus, his mother, and his closest friends had arrived in Cana at the very beginning, when the groom had claimed his betrothed from her father's house and escorted her to his father's house. There, under a flower-laden canopy, a *huppa*, they became husband and wife and retreated to the room the groom had added to his father's house. When the groom appeared once more to announce to the wedding guests that the marriage had been consummated, the feasting and drinking and dancing began in earnest.

After that, the newlyweds remained secluded while the guests par-tied on. Jesus ate and drank and danced with all the others. The groom's parents, who were related to Jesus' mother, Mary,[136] had spent months preparing for the occasion, which would last seven days. Family mem-bers, servants, and neighbors worked around the clock to keep the food and wine flowing to the guests, who sang and danced each night until the wee hours and then slept on the ground under the stars.

Midway through the feast, Mary approached her son with a grim expression. She waited for Elihud the butcher, a cousin of theirs, to finish telling a story and then knelt next to Jesus, who half-reclined on the ground between John bar Zebedee and Simon bar Jonas. She placed a hand on his shoulder and placed her lips close to his ear. "They have no more wine," she said.

He sighed. "Dear woman, why do you involve me? My hour has not yet come."

Mary said nothing, but fastened a pleading gaze on him. They both knew the shame that would befall the groom and his family if the provisions ran out before the feast ended. The celebration would end prematurely. Many guests would go home. The bride and groom would be dishonored, and the family would be pitied or scorned for many years to come.

An observer would not have noticed the silent transaction between mother and son, but when Mary stood and walked away, she went straight to the servants who had first noticed the shortage of wine. She gestured in Jesus' direction. "Do whatever he tells you."

Within moments, Jesus slipped away from his friends and followers, some of whom followed him with their eyes. He approached the servants. He nodded to six massive stone water jars nearby. "Fill the jars with water."

The servants exchanged the briefest of glances with each other, but they moved quickly to obey. When the jars were full, Jesus issued further instructions. "Now draw some out and take it to the master of the banquet."

The servants blinked, as if they awaited a punch line. But when Jesus simply nodded, one of the servants stepped forward, dipped a cup in the closest jar, and walked away. Jesus turned and headed back to his friends. The feast would go on, uninterrupted. The six stone jars were filled. Twenty gallons each. Of the finest wine the earth had ever seen.

Jesus Kept the Party Going

When John the beloved disciple recorded the miracle at Cana in his Gospel (the only Gospel writer to mention this remarkable event), he concluded his account, "This, the first of his signs, Jesus did at Cana in Galilee, and manifested his glory. And his disciples believed in him."[137] A great finish to a memorable story. But he didn't have to end it that way. He could just as easily have concluded the story this way: "Jesus' first miracle kept the party going."

His words to his mother seem to indicate that Jesus' first miracle wasn't planned, much less calculated to reveal his identity or establish his authority. In fact, John's account leaves the impression that the wedding guests—other than his mother and his disciples—didn't even know about the miracle. But he did it, nonetheless. Perhaps out of love for his mother. Maybe also to prevent the newlyweds and their family from being embarrassed. In any case, his actions served one more purpose: to keep the party going.

Jesus' contemporaries saw him as a party animal. He never sinned, but the Bible never depicts him as a wet blanket at a party. Exactly the opposite, in fact. From all appearances, Jesus loved a good party. Matthew's Gospel records: "While Jesus was having dinner at Matthew's house, many tax collectors and 'sinners' came and ate with him and his disciples. When the Pharisees saw this, they asked his disciples, 'Why does your teacher eat with tax collectors and 'sinners'?'"[138]

Jesus knew full well what his opponents were saying about him, but that never stopped him from going to parties and hanging out with the "wrong" crowd: "The Son of Man came eating and drinking, and they say, 'Here is a glutton and a drunkard, a friend of tax collectors and sinners.' But wisdom is proved right by her actions."[139]

Jesus was not a glutton or a drunkard. But he knew how to have a good time, and he often enjoyed a good time with the "wrong" types— who, by the way, clearly enjoyed being around him. He certainly had a gift for storytelling. He knew how to keep a party going. He was probably even the life of the party: witty, charming, and fun.

The Kingdom of God Is a Party

Most of us, though we call ourselves followers of Jesus, are not much like him in that respect. And we do not ordinarily think of the kingdom of God and the things of God the way Jesus did. If we did, we would tend to act more like him. We might be accused of being party animals instead of (as Christians are sometimes perceived and portrayed) as party poopers.

Have you ever stopped to consider how Jesus pictured the kingdom of God? Have you ever compared your perceptions of this kingdom with his?

Luke 14 contains one such depiction. It is called Jesus' Parable of the Great Banquet. In it, he portrays the kingdom of God as a banquet. A party. A seven-day feast. In other words, in Jesus' mind, the kingdom of God is synonymous with a wild and crazy good time.

> When one of those at the table with [Jesus] heard [his teaching], he said to Jesus, "Blessed is the man who will eat at the feast in the kingdom of God."
>
> Jesus replied: "A certain man was preparing a great banquet and invited many guests. At the time of the banquet he sent his servant to tell those who had been invited, 'Come, for everything is now ready.'
>
> "But they all alike began to make excuses. . . . [So] the servant came back and reported this to his master. Then the owner of the house became angry and ordered his servant, 'Go out

quickly into the streets and alleys of the town and bring in the poor, the crippled, the blind and the lame.'

"'Sir,' the servant said, 'what you ordered has been done, but there is still room.'

"Then the master told his servant, 'Go out to the roads and country lanes and make them come in, so that my house will be full.'"[140]

Does that sound like church to you? It should. Because that's how Jesus sees it. To him, the kingdom of God is a feast, a banquet, a party. A soirée. A blast. A ball. A blowout. A shindig. A hootenanny, even.

Honestly, I'm convinced Jesus is bored with many of our church "fellowship" events . . . when he's not broken-hearted. Not that he minds serene or sedate church gatherings. A great party doesn't have to be loud, but it is always fun. And too often, what we call "fellowship" in the church today wouldn't have made a decent funeral in Jesus' day.

Having Too Much Fun

Do you remember the story of the birth of the church?

Jesus had risen from the dead and ascended into heaven. He had told his closest followers to pray and wait for the promised Holy Spirit to come upon them. So they did, and thus they were all together when the Feast of Pentecost arrived.

Notice: the *Feast* of Pentecost.

Pentecost—or *Shavuot*—was the annual party in which the Jews gave thanks and presented offerings for the summer wheat harvest in Israel. Work ceased. Food and drink abounded. Tens of thousands of people from near and far journeyed to Jerusalem to celebrate together. They sat around campfires under the summer sun and sang. They danced. They gathered in the temple courts and reunited with family and friends.

At this very time, Jesus' closest friends were together. The sound of a mighty wind rushed through the windows and filled the house where they were gathered. A ball of fire appeared in the room and separated into tongues of flame that seemed to rest on every person's head, they were filled with the Holy Spirit, and they became aware that they were suddenly able to speak in other languages.

They must have made their way out of the house and into the streets together, for before long they were amid a crowd of people. The crowd grew, as people from distant lands heard these Galilean rubes rejoicing and shouting the praises of God in their own languages. The commotion continued. Jews from all over the world—Greece, Rome, Egypt, Arabia, Asia—looked on in amazement at this clamor of languages coming from the followers of Jesus.

As the crowd grew and became more amazed and more restless, do you remember what they said? What they assumed? What they surmised was going on?

Take a moment to consider what the crowd did *not* say. They did not say, "These people are angry."

They did not say, "These people hate us."

They did not say, "These people are boring."

They did not say, "These people are crazy."

No. They didn't say any such thing. You remember, don't you? They said, "They're drunk on sweet wine!"[141]

Why? Why did the crowd say they were drunk? What was it in the disciples' behavior that prompted such a response?

Because they were "declaring the wonders of God"?[142] I doubt it, because these were all observant Jews who had gathered to give thanks to God. It is unlikely they would have been shocked to hear another group of Jews praising God out loud.

Because they were speaking in many different languages? Probably not, because drunkenness tends to make people *less* articulate, not more so.

What was it, then? What made the crowd make fun of the disciples by saying they were drunk?

I think it was this: they were having way too much fun to believe they were sober.

I think these followers of Jesus burst out in public with such uncontainable joy and laughter that observers thought potent wine had to be involved somehow. I think the followers of Jesus, who had been cowering in seclusion just fifty days before, were having themselves a party in the public square. In fact, the context doesn't require us to think the disciples left the house to go evangelizing that day; they appear to have just spilled out spontaneously, having such a blast that crowds began to gather. And we're told that three thousand people joined the church on that first day.

And I think *that* is a further fulfillment of what Jesus had in mind when he told the story of the Great Banquet. I think Acts 2 is the realization of what Jesus showed us: the kingdom of God is a party. In fact, when that same chapter of Acts says those first Christians "devoted themselves to the apostles' teaching and to the fellowship,"[143] I think the word fellowship (*koinonia* in the Greek) describes something more akin to an ongoing block party than to the coffees and potlucks that we have grown accustomed to in the church.

A Wee Hours Birthday Party

Tony Campolo often tells the story of a memorable visit to Honolulu. In 2009, he told it like this at the Crystal Cathedral in Garden Grove, California:

I had to go to speak in Honolulu. Well, sometimes you get L.A. and sometimes you get Honolulu. If you go to Honolulu, because of the distance from the east coast where I live, there's a six-hour time difference. And I woke up at about three o'clock in the morning and I was hungry and I wanted to get something to eat. But, in a hustling city like Honolulu at three o'clock in the morning, it's hard to find anything that's open. Up a side street, I spotted this greasy spoon, and I went in. It was one of these dirty places and they didn't have any booths, just a row of stools at the counter. I sat down a bit uneasy and I didn't touch the menu. It was one of those plastic menus and grease had piled up on it. I knew that if I opened it, something extraterrestrial would have crawled out. All of the sudden, this very heavy-set, unshaved man with a cigar came out of the back room, put down his cigar, and said, "What do you want?" I said, "I'd like a cup of coffee and a donut."

He poured the coffee and then he scratched himself and, with the same hand, picked up the donut. I hate that. So, there I am, three-thirty in the morning, drinking my coffee, and eating this dirty donut. And into the place comes about eight or nine prostitutes. It's a small place, they sit on either side of me, and I tried to disappear. The woman on my immediate right was very boisterous and she said to her friend, "Tomorrow's my birthday. I'm going to be thirty-nine."

Her friend said, "So what do you want me to do? Do you want me to sing happy birthday? Should we have a cake a party? It's your birthday."

The first woman said, "Look, why do you have to put me down? I've never had a birthday party in my whole life. I don't expect to have one now."

That's all I needed. I waited until they left and I called Harry over and I asked, "Do they come in here every night?"

He said, "Yes."

I said, "The one right next to me . . ."

"Agnes."

"Tomorrow is her birthday. What do you think about decorating the place? When she comes in tomorrow night, we'll throw a birthday party for her. What do you think?"

He said, "Mister, that is brilliant. That is brilliant!" He called his wife out of the back room. "Jan, come out here. I want you to meet this guy. He wants to throw a birthday party for Agnes."

She came out and took my hand and squeezed it tightly, and said, "You wouldn't understand this, mister, but Agnes is one of the good people, one of the kind people in this town. And nobody ever does anything for her, and this is a good thing."

I said, "Can I decorate the place?"

She said, "To your heart's content."

I said, "I'm going to bring a birthday cake."

Harry said, "Oh no! The cake's my thing!"

So, I got there the next morning at about two-thirty. I had bought the streamers at the K-mart, strung them about the place. I had made a big poster—"Happy Birthday Agnes"—and put it behind the counter. I had the place spruced up. Everything was set. Everything was ready. Jan, who does the cooking, she had gotten the word out on the street. By three-fifteen, every prostitute was squeezed into this diner. People, it was wall-to-wall prostitutes and me!

Three-thirty in the morning, in come Agnes and her friends. I've got everybody set, everybody ready. As they come through the door, we all yell, "Happy birthday Agnes!" In addition, we start cheering like mad. I've never seen anybody so stunned. Her knees buckled. They steadied her and sat her down on the stool. We all started singing, "Happy birthday, happy birthday, happy birthday to you!"

When they brought out the cake, she lost it and started to cry. Harry just stood there with the cake and said, "All right, knock it off Agnes. Blow out the candles. Come on, blow out the candles." She tried, but she couldn't, so he blew out the candles, gave her the knife, and said, "Cut the cake, Agnes."

She sat there for a long moment and then she said to me, "Mister, is it okay if I don't cut the cake? What I'd like to do, mister, is take the cake home and show it to my mother. Could I do that?"

I said, "It's your cake." She stood up, and I said, "Do you have to do it now?"

She said, "I live two doors down. Let me take the cake home and show it to my mother. I promise you I'll bring it right back." And she moved toward the door carrying the cake as though it was the Holy Grail. As she pushed through the crowd and out the door, the door swung slowly shut and there was stunned silence. You talk about an awkward moment. Everyone was motionless. Everyone was still [and] I didn't know what to say.

So, I finally said, "What do you say, we pray?" It's weird looking back on it now. You know a sociologist leading a prayer meeting with a bunch of prostitutes at three-thirty in the morning in a diner. But, it was the right thing to do. I prayed that God would deliver her from what dirty filthy men had done to her. You know how these things start—some ten, eleven, or twelve-year-old girl gets messed over and destroyed by some filthy man and then she goes downhill from there. And men use her and abuse her. I said, "God, deliver her and make her into a new creation because I've got a God who can make us new no matter where we've been or what we've been through." And I prayed that God would make her new.

When I finished my prayer, Harry leaned over the counter and he said, "Campolo, you told me you were a sociologist. You're no sociologist, you're a preacher. What kind of church do you belong to?"

In one of those moments when you come up with just the right words, I said, "I belong to a church that throws birthday parties for whores at three-thirty in the morning."

I'll never forget his response. He looked back at me and he said, "No you don't, no you don't. I would join a church like that!"

Wouldn't we all? Wouldn't we all like to belong to a church that threw birthday parties for whores at three-thirty in the morning? Well, I've got news for you. That is the kind of church that Jesus came to create. He came to bring celebration into people's lives that have had nothing to celebrate. This is true religion, says the epistle of James, to visit the fatherless, the widows, and the afflicted and bring celebration into their lives. He is the Christ who saves you from sin and fills you with his joy, commissions you to go out and to spread that joy to the world because the Lord has come.[144]

Let's Learn How to Party

Tony Campolo has it right. I think Agnes's birthday party was much closer to the "fellowship" of the church than all the church suppers I've been to combined. That's why I say, "Quit fellowshipping . . . and party instead." Let's heed what Rob Bell says: "I am learning that the church has nothing to say to the world until it throws better parties."[145] Let's learn how to throw such enjoyable parties—as individuals, families, and churches—that others will sit up and take notice, crowds will begin to form, others will want to join us, and some might even say, "I would join a church like that."

Never forget that when Jesus was accused of being a glutton and a drunkard, it was members of the religious establishment pronouncing judgment on him for rubbing shoulders with the "wrong" sorts of people. And remember, when the freshly Spirit-filled followers of Jesus spilled out into the streets of Jerusalem on the day of Pentecost, thousands of people were infected by their impromptu block party. And imagine what will happen when the church—*your* church—becomes known throughout your community as a bunch of people who know how to party and who bring celebration into people's lives who have had nothing to celebrate. It might not please all the religious folk. But it will attract "the poor, the crippled, the blind and the lame."[146] And it will please God, the Master of the Banquet.

~§ *Prayer*

Abba, Father, make me a party animal . . . like Jesus, your Son.

Make me like Jesus, who knew how to have fun.

Make me like Jesus, who knew how to keep a party going.

Make me like Jesus, who included the sick, suffering, and sinful in his fun.

Make me like Jesus, who sees the kingdom of God as a party.

Make me like Jesus, who was always a gracious guest and maybe even the life of the party.

Fill me with your Spirit. Fill me to overflowing, that his joy might live in me and flow from me, until the people around me are tempted to say, "What have you been drinking?"

In Jesus' name, Amen.

CHAPTER TEN

Quit Trying to Be Good

My mother used to collect American silver half-dollars.

And I used to steal them.

I'm ashamed to admit it, of course, but it's true. I don't recall at exactly what age kleptomania first struck. I was younger than thirteen, because I distinctly remember—to this day—the dresser drawer in her bedroom in our house in Cincinnati, where she kept the half-dollars, and we moved out of that house in my thirteenth year.

I thought I was being clever by taking only one or two half-dollars at a time, making sure I consumed the pack of Razzles gum, French Twist or Fun Dip candy, or ice-cold Pepsi, and disposing of the evidence before she came home from work. It turned out, however, that my mom could count. I guess I hadn't planned things as perfectly as I thought. (I'm a little brighter these days, but not by much.)

The discovery of my perfidy devastated me. I cried. I promised to make restitution, something I knew would take a long time, since I didn't receive an allowance and had no job. (I had long before quit my career as delivery boy for a weekly neighborhood newspaper because I somehow managed to spend more on rubber bands than I ever collected in subscriptions.) But I knew it would take even longer to restore my mother's trust in me.

Thing is, each time I pilfered from my mom's half-dollar collection, I vowed it would be my last. I knew it was wrong. I knew it was sinful. I knew I would get caught, sooner or later. I repeatedly promised myself—and God—that I would "go straight," that I would stop stealing half-dollars before it led to worse crimes, like robbing banks and liquor stores. But I never did. Until I got caught.

That pattern repeated itself many times in my life. When I was fourteen, my mom died of breast cancer. In the weeks and months following her funeral, I grieved, of course. Mostly alone. I descended into a deep depression. I didn't know at the time what was going on; I just knew I had no interest in much of anything. Certainly not school. To say I had trouble focusing on school would be like saying the Cyclops had trouble crossing his eye. So I stopped going.

For two and a half years after my mother's death, I skipped so much school I was branded with the nickname AWOL by my freshman biology teacher, Mr. Phillips. He would call my name in class and add the comment, "AWOL again." After awhile, none of my classmates even knew my first name.

I refined truancy to an art form. I became adept at lying, at forging absence excuses in my father's handwriting, at falsifying report cards, and at creating clever—but credible—stories when school officials would call on the phone during the day (when my father was at work). I screened the mail every day to filter anything that threatened to disrupt my career as a truant, and I reviewed the school lunch menus in the newspaper each week, in case Dad would happen to ask what I'd had for lunch that day.

And the thing is, just like before, I knew I was messing up. I knew I needed to go back to school. I knew it would catch up with me. For two and a half years, I would go to bed every Friday night vowing to myself—and to God—that Monday morning I would "go straight." I would go back to school. But I never did. Until I got caught.

Not by the school. Not by my dad. Truth is, my girlfriend found out and informed me that our relationship more or less depended on me not becoming a street person. So I straightened up. I buckled down. I started back to school. And I squeezed four years of high school into the next two and a half, finishing just in time for my wedding—to that girl.

Something's Wrong Inside

We all do it. I do it; you do it. We try to be good.

Especially those of us who have experienced forgiveness and new life through faith in Jesus Christ. More than ever before, we want to please God. We want to do right. We want to avoid sin. But we don't. Until we get caught.

A long time ago, a guy named Paul wrote the definitive description of such efforts. He said, "I can will it, but I can't do it. I decide to do good, but I don't really do it; I decide not to do bad, but then I do it anyway. My decisions, such as they are, don't result in actions. Something has gone wrong deep within me and gets the better of me every time."[147]

This whole "trying to be good" thing is a waste of time. So I suggest we stop. Quit trying to be good. It doesn't work. Worse than that, it is counterproductive.

"Well, now, pull back on those reins, cowpoke," you might say (if you sound a lot like John Wayne when you talk). Isn't the whole idea of the Christian life kind of trying to be good? Overcoming our sins? Becoming victorious over temptation? Living righteous lives? Isn't that what it's all about? Isn't that the whole point?

Nope.

Not even close.

That is a common misconception, but the fact that it is common does not make it any less false.

Steve McVey of Grace Walk Ministries writes:

> Trying to overcome sin by focusing on it has the exact opposite effect of what we want in our lives. If we fixate on what we do wrong and try to figure out how to conquer the bad behavior, we will always come up with some sort of plan that involves our own willpower and determination. When that happens, it doesn't matter how sincere we might be. We are setting ourselves up to fail.[148]

This is not an easy thing for human beings to grasp. It is like the Vulcan death grip or the concept of the Force in the *Star Wars* movies. It doesn't jibe with our accustomed way of thinking or acting. It's counterintuitive. It's not natural to us. It is *super*natural.

How to Be Righteous without Really Trying

The same guy Paul who wrote about how useless it is to try to be good also wrote a letter to a group of churches in a region called Galatia. This two-thousand-year-old letter is preserved today in our Bibles under the title *Galatians*. Paul wrote it because many of those good churchgoing people had started to believe that their faith in Jesus Christ was valid *only if* they were *also* careful to live by the traditions and regulations and rules that had characterized Judaism for generations.

So Paul wrote this letter to tell them, "That is *not* what it means to follow Jesus. You are free from all that." But being free from the law does not mean that once we've received the grace of God and experienced the forgiveness of sins, we're just all going to run wild like some drug-induced hippie love-in. No, the freedom we have in Christ, our freedom from the burden of the law, our freedom from slavery to sin, ought to result—*can* result—in *more* righteousness and holiness than we could ever manufacture *by trying to be good*.

Sounds good, right? But how, you might wonder. How is that supposed to work? How can we live righteous and holy lives without trying? We don't have to wonder, because Paul actually explained it, long ago. He said:

> Live by the Spirit, and you will not gratify the desires of the sinful nature. For the sinful nature desires what is contrary to the Spirit, and the Spirit what is contrary to the sinful nature. They are in conflict with each other, so that you do not do what you want. But if you are led by the Spirit, you are not under law.
>
> The acts of the sinful nature are obvious: sexual immorality, impurity and debauchery; idolatry and witchcraft; hatred, discord, jealousy, fits of rage, selfish ambition, dissensions, factions and envy; drunkenness, orgies, and the like. I warn you, as I did before, that those who live like this will not inherit the kingdom of God.
>
> But the fruit of the Spirit is love, joy, peace, patience, kindness, goodness, faithfulness, gentleness and self-control. Against such things there is no law. Those who belong to Christ Jesus

have crucified the sinful nature with its passions and desires. Since we live by the Spirit, let us keep in step with the Spirit. . . .

Do not be deceived: God cannot be mocked. A man reaps what he sows. The one who sows to please his sinful nature, from that nature will reap destruction; the one who sows to please the Spirit, from the Spirit will reap eternal life.[149]

Interesting, isn't it, how some of Paul's words in that passage parallel what he said in Romans 7 about trying to be good and do right? But in his letter to the Galatian churches, he gets more specific about how we're supposed to live righteous and holy lives without trying. He says, "Live by the Spirit and you will not gratify the desires of the sinful nature."

He says, "If you are led by the Spirit, you are not under law."

He says, "But the fruit of the Spirit is love, joy, peace . . ."

And finally, "Since we live by the Spirit, let us keep in step with the Spirit."

You see that, right? He's on to something. He's making a point and hammering it home. And the point is this: the new life Christians have been given, the fruit we ought to be producing, is not called "the fruit of my efforts." It is called "the fruit of the Spirit."

That truth is inexpressibly important. It's the nexus, the core of a whole new way of thinking and acting. It is so contrary to human nature, so unlike the way we tend to talk and think and act, that I believe even Paul himself lacks the language to put it perfectly, to fully express it without making it sound like it still depends on my effort. Which is why I think he says, over and over again:

"live by the Spirit"
"keep in step with the Spirit"
"be led by the Spirit"

It's not natural. It's *super*natural.

It's not an effort thing. It's a Spirit thing.

It's not a new command. It's a non-command.

It's not one more thing you have to do. It's the only thing.

Beyond Behavior Modification

In the last few generations, at least, Christians have become known for all the stuff we're against. "We don't smoke, we don't chew, we don't go out with girls who do." We steer clear of "cigarettes, whiskey, and wild, wild women." That kinda stuff.

And for longer than I've been alive—which is a really long time—Christians and churches have focused a lot of energy on behavior modification. You know, if you're going to be a Christian:

You gotta quit drugs.

You gotta quit alcohol.

You gotta quit sleeping around.

You gotta quit cheating and stealing and lying . . .

because that's what being a "Christian" is all about, right?

Wrong.

That's not what the Christ life is about. That's not what it means to follow Jesus. Because if I could do all that, *I wouldn't need Jesus.* I could be my *own* Savior. And a lot of people *are* (or try to be). A lot of people are living by the rules, not by the Spirit. Which looks on the surface like a good thing. But it's not.

That Paul guy told the Galatian Christians, "All who rely on observing the law are under a curse."[150]

That can't be good.

He then goes on to string together four Old Testament Scriptures to make his case, using them to connect Abraham to Jesus in four easy steps, sort of like the Kevin Bacon game:

> All who rely on observing the law are under a curse, for it is written: "Cursed is everyone who does not continue to do everything written in the Book of the Law." Clearly no one is justified before God by the law, because, "The righteous will live by faith." The law is not based on faith; on the contrary, "The man who does these things will live by them." Christ redeemed us from the curse of the law by becoming a curse for us, for it is written: "Cursed is everyone who is hung on a tree." He redeemed us in order that the blessing given to Abraham might come to the Gentiles through Christ Jesus, so that by faith we might receive the promise of the Spirit.[151]

It is by trusting in Christ that we enter the kingdom of God, it is by trusting in Christ that we receive the promise of the Spirit, and it is by trusting in Christ that we live the Christian life.

We do not achieve holiness by gritting our teeth and trying to be good. That is a recipe for disappointment and disaster. It happens only as the result of something Scotsman Thomas Chalmers famously called, "The expulsive power of a new affection." We don't talk like that anymore, but the phrase basically means that when a new affection, a new passion, a new love enters a person's heart and life, it drives out—expels—everything in its path.

She Left Her Water Jug

Remember the woman at the well?

Jesus was on his way through a region called Samaria. He and his band of followers arrived outside a town called Sychar, known far and wide for its location near the plot of land the patriarch Jacob had given to his son Joseph.

They'd walked since dawn. It was noon. Jesus was tired. He stopped at the well outside the town, which everyone called "Jacob's well," and sent his entourage into the town to buy food.

The woman arrived soon after. Alone—which, together with the time of day, spoke volumes about her status and reputation. She eyed the strange man but said nothing as she lowered her jug into the well.

He spoke first. "Will you give me a drink of water?"

She answered without lifting her gaze from what she was doing. "You are a Jew and I am a Samaritan woman. How can you ask me for a drink?"

They both knew the taboos. As a Jew, he had already broken several. Traveling through—instead of around—Samaria. Speaking to a woman. Having anything to do with a Samaritan—let alone someone of such obvious low repute. Would he also drink from the cup of an "unclean" person?

"If you knew the gift of God and who it is that asks you for a drink, you would have asked him and he would have given you living water."

She lifted her jar out of the well and set it on the ground. Her tone was weary, almost impatient. "Sir, you have nothing to draw with and the well is deep. Where can you get this living water? Are you greater than our father Jacob, who gave us the well and drank from it himself, as did also his sons and his flocks and herds?"

"Everyone who drinks this water will be thirsty again, but whoever drinks the water I give him will never thirst. Indeed, the water I give him will become in him a spring of water welling up to eternal life."

She finally looked at him and was surprised at the gracious smile he wore. "Sir, give me this water so that I won't get thirsty and have to keep coming here to draw water."[152]

As the story continues, the woman learns not only that this Jewish man accepts her instead of rejecting her and judging her as she would have expected; she learns that he actually claims to be the promised Messiah, the Son of God, who knows all about her . . . and still accepts her. So, when Jesus' followers returned from their foray into town, the Bible records:

"Then, leaving her water jar, the woman went back to the town and said to the people, 'Come, see a man who told me everything I ever did. Could this be the Christ?' They came out of the town and made their way toward him."[153]

That woman came to the well . . . for water. She brought a big ol' water jar with her, intending to carry it back home with a fresh supply, for drinking and cooking and washing. It was her habit, it was ingrained, it was part and parcel of her daily lifestyle. Yet she totally left her water jar there, by the well, when she ran back into town.

Nobody told her to "leave that old thing behind." No one said, "Here's how you have to act if you want to be this man's follower." There was no class on "how to share your faith with others."

But when she met Jesus, when she experienced his presence, when she learned who he claimed to be and what he said he could do, she didn't need advice. She didn't need willpower. She just left it sitting there because—in an instant—her plans, perspective, and priorities had all changed.

The expulsive power of a new affection.

He Left His Greed

Ever hear of Zacchaeus?

He was a little man. In more than one way.

He lived in Jericho, where he served the Roman occupiers by collecting taxes from his neighbors. Like others in his line of work, he became wealthy by skimming more than a little off the top. He probably compensated for his small physical stature by flaunting his wealth among his neighbors.

Then Jesus entered his life.

Zacchaeus had heard of the Galilean rabbi, the controversial healer. So when he heard that Jesus was coming to Jericho, he ventured out to see him. But a crowd had gathered for the same reason. Everyone wanted to see Jesus. They lined the street. Shoulder-to-shoulder. Elbow-to-elbow. Even three or four people deep.

Do you think any of Zacchaeus's neighbors—or victims, if you like— would step aside to let in the little man? Not a chance. At the tax man's approach, the crowd tightened, and gaps closed.

But Zacchaeus hadn't gotten to where he was by taking no for an answer. He spied a tall sycamore tree and ran to it. He climbed the tree. He was in time. He saw the dusty rabbi approaching, with his *talmidim* following closely behind.

> When Jesus reached the spot, he looked up and said to him, "Zacchaeus, come down immediately. I must stay at your house today." So he came down at once and welcomed him gladly.
>
> All the people saw this and began to mutter, "He has gone to be the guest of a 'sinner.'"
>
> But Zacchaeus stood up and said to the Lord, "Look, Lord! Here and now I give half of my possessions to the poor, and if

I have cheated anybody out of anything, I will pay back four times the amount."

Jesus said to him, "Today salvation has come to this house, because this man, too, is a son of Abraham. For the Son of Man came to seek and to save what was lost."[154]

Now, you gotta understand. Zacchaeus was not some cute Sunday school flannel cutout. He was the picture of corruption. An extortionist. Think *mobster*. He'd built his fortune on the backs of innocent people.

And yet when he saw Jesus, and Jesus saw him, something changed. Somehow, sometime in their interaction, as they sat and ate together in Zacchaeus's house, Jesus reached into that man's heart and changed him so completely that his greed, his avarice, and his materialism apparently evaporated.

Suddenly, this man who had *lived his life for money* pulled out his checkbook like Scrooge on Christmas morning.

Nobody told him to "stop cheating people." Nobody said, "Here's how you have to act if you want to be this man's follower." Nobody asked him for a donation.

But when he met Jesus and experienced his presence, his acceptance, and his love, all he had once held dear seemed unimportant.

The expulsive power of a new affection.

She Left Her Demons

And then there was Mary, a woman with a common name and a decidedly uncommon past: "After this, Jesus traveled about from one town and village to another, proclaiming the good news of the kingdom of God. The Twelve were with him, and also some women who had been cured of evil spirits and diseases: Mary (called Magdalene) from whom seven demons had come out."[155]

Mark's account is a tad more precise, specifying that it was Jesus who freed her from those seven demons. But you probably already figured that.

It was that same Mary who followed Jesus up and down the roads of Galilee and Judea. It was that same Mary who stood at the cross and watched Jesus die when nearly everyone else deserted him. The same Mary who helped prepare his body for burial. The same Mary who came early that first Easter morning to the tomb, and the same Mary who became the first evangelist in history, when the risen Jesus told her to go and tell the others that he was alive.

Do you think someone had to tell her, "Go where Jesus goes?" You think somebody had to say, "Do what Jesus says?" You think anyone instructed her, "See what Jesus thinks?" Don't you think when you've been freed from seven demons you might experience "the expulsive power of a new affection"?

I think so.

When she met Jesus, she left her demons behind.

I think we get way too focused on not doing wrong things. I know I do. I think we even get way too focused on trying to do the right things. Even that misses the mark. Because our focus needs to be on *one thing*.

Just One Thing

There was a day, recorded in Scripture, when Jesus came to the home of two sisters named Mary and Martha. Martha set to work cleaning and cooking and getting everything right. But Mary, her sister, never tied on her apron. Never swept the floor. Didn't wash a single cucumber or tomato. Left the stoking of the fire in the bake oven to someone—anyone—else.

Mary sat herself down in the presence of Jesus and watched him closely and listened closely and stayed right there.

Before long, Martha came, all sweaty and frazzled, cheeks red from the heat of the oven, flour dust in her hair, wiping her hands on her apron, and she said to Jesus, "Lord, don't you care that my sister has left me to do the work by myself? Tell her to help me!"

Jesus answered, "Martha, Martha . . . you are worried and upset about many things, but only one thing is needed. Mary has chosen what is better, and it will not be taken away from her."[156]

One thing, Jesus said.

One thing.

"The expulsive power of a new affection."

A Daily Focus

I don't know how messed up your life is. I don't care how many bad habits you have. It doesn't matter how many issues you have to deal with. Only one thing is needed: "the expulsive power of a new affection."

You will not clean up your act by gritting your teeth and trying hard. You will not improve yourself by willpower. You will not attain holiness by being worried and upset about any number of things. Only one thing is needed: the expulsive power of a new affection.

If you would leave your water jar, or your money bags, or your demons behind, only one thing is needed. If you focus on quitting a habit or overcoming a sin, your focus is all wrong. If you concentrate on saying no to temptation, your focus is all wrong. You can be changed only by the expulsive power of a new affection.

All our efforts, all our willpower, all our determination amounts to nothing. It is all garbage . . . compared to the thing that happens when we turn our eyes on Jesus, when we rediscover his love for us and our love for him, when we focus on *one thing*.

One thing.

Being in his presence,
sitting at his feet,
surrendering to him,
worshipping him,
gazing on his face,
spending time in his presence,
seeking him,
loving him,
talking to him,
listening to him.

Every day one thing is needed.

Every day you have only one temptation to avoid: the temptation to neglect that one thing.

Every day you have nothing better to do than to turn your eyes on Jesus, look full on his wonderful face, experience his presence and power, and then—then the things of earth will grow strangely dim. You'll forget your water jug. You'll overcome your greed. You'll experience deliverance.

It won't be something *you* make happen. It won't be the result of teeth-gritting effort. It will simply be "the expulsive power of a new affection."

~~∽ *Prayer*

Father, please make it so in my life. Let the love of Jesus fill me and drive far from me every undesirable thing. Save me from placing any faith in my own teeth-gritting, willpower-exercising ability to "be good." Deliver me from any expectation that I can effectively modify my behavior enough to produce love, joy, peace, patience, kindness, goodness, faithfulness, gentleness, or self-control in my life. Free me from the lie that I can be a "good Christian."

Instead, Father, help me to focus every day on one thing and one thing alone: to sit at the feet of my Lord, surrender to him, focus on him, worship him, gaze on his face, dwell in his presence, seeking him, loving him, talking to him, and listening to him. And then let me keep in step with his Spirit in this way through each day, in Jesus' name. Amen.

CHAPTER ELEVEN

Quit Enjoying Worship

Picture your place of worship. It may be a quaint country chapel with well-polished wooden pews. Or a cavernous cathedral, massive and magnificent. Or perhaps it is a state-of-the-art auditorium featuring a projection screen the size of a Balkan nation. Or something else.

In any case, put yourself there, in that place, in your imagination. The worship service has just ended. People are lingering, hugging, milling around, filing out, smiling, laughing, and talking to each other.

"Wasn't worship wonderful today?" someone might say.

"Don't you love music like that?" another may add.

"I really liked the sermon today."

"Me too, and isn't the pastor totally dreamy?" (Hey, it could happen. Not at my church, but it could happen somewhere.)

Those would be typical comments, right? Maybe more positive than some, but fairly common, nonetheless.

And totally beside the point.

I'm not saying those things are unimportant; I'm saying none of those people are talking about worship.

It's one thing when newcomers to the church say such things, but it's something else entirely when supposedly mature Christ-followers approach worship primarily from the standpoint of such questions as:

Does it meet my needs?

Fit my style?

Lift my soul?

Inspire me?

Fill me?

Fulfill me?

Thrill me?

True worship can certainly do all those things, but thinking and speaking of worship in those terms ought to jar us. Because that's not worship.

Every Which Way of Worship

I have been privileged to participate in worship in all kinds of settings. As I mentioned in the first chapter, I estimate that I have gone to church more than five thousand times in my lifetime—so far. That's five thousand worship services. Five thousand.

I have worshipped to the accompaniment of a forty-piece brass band in a crowded Salvation Army chapel. I have bowed my head by campfire light in a grove of trees at a Christian camp. I have wept with the joy of the Lord in a pueblo worship service in Arequipa, Peru. I have praised God to the tune of a single guitar as the sun set on a picturesque beach. I have listened to gripping, tearful testimonies of deliverance in a skid-row mission church. I have sung "He Lives" at the Garden Tomb in Jerusalem and worshipped while afloat on the Sea of Galilee. I have joined the procession in a historic Episcopal church, attended a three-hour-long liturgy and ordination service in a Greek Orthodox church, and celebrated 3 A.M. vigils with Trappist monks in a Roman Catholic monastery.

One of the most memorable sermons I've ever heard was preached on Hebrews 12:6 ("The Lord disciplines those he loves"). I was attending church with my brother-in-law, Ron, on a sizzling August day in Cincinnati, Ohio. Some folks might have come to church that day to escape the heat in the air-conditioned sanctuary; unfortunately, the air conditioner had broken down during the night. Sitting shoulder-to-shoulder in the crowded sanctuary, we sweated through the service. When the time for the sermon arrived, there was not a dry shirt or blouse in the place. But the preacher showed admirable wisdom and sensitivity. "If it is true," he began, "that the Lord disciplines those he loves, and if it is true that oppressive heat may be a form of discipline, then the Lord must love us very, very much. Go in peace." With that, he concluded. I nearly gave the man a standing ovation. And I could tell I was not alone in my appreciation.

Another unforgettable experience was in upstate New York, when my wife and I were "cadets" in training for ministry in the Salvation Army. We were conducting services in a storefront chapel in an urban area. The preacher for the morning had just stepped into the pulpit when a woman stood up from her seat in the back of the chapel. She walked slowly down the center aisle toward the altar, prompting us to rejoice that the Spirit had apparently moved this woman to come forward for prayer long before any altar call had been issued. But she didn't kneel at the altar. She made her way onto the platform and disappeared through a side door—which was the only available restroom in the building. As distracting as that was, the preacher somehow managed to keep going without losing too much momentum. Until, that is, a tremulous female voice came through that door on the platform, announcing, "There's no toilet paper in here!"

One of the most arresting worship experiences of my life, however, was not in a church service at all, but in a church leadership meeting. The leaders of the church my wife and I had planted (with four others) in Oxford, Ohio, were gathered in a community meeting room to pray about the acquisition of land for a future campus. As we united in prayer, the Holy Spirit descended on that group and moved through the room with mighty power. Soon we were all weeping and praising God for his manifest presence. Perhaps no one was more surprised than I was when a church business meeting turned into a worship experience.

It Ain't about You

Worship is not in the least about meeting my needs, fitting your style, or lifting our souls. Whether it fills me, fulfills me, or thrills me is entirely beside the point. As television's Dr. Phil is famously prone to say, "It ain't about you."

We tend to make it about us. We choose a church based on whether we *like* the music or the preaching. We evaluate a worship service based on whether we were moved or inspired. We even talk about Sunday worship as a critical spiritual "shot in the arm" that meets our needs by getting us through the rest of the week.

I suggest we cut it out. We need to stop such talk. We should banish such thoughts from our minds and thoroughly transform how we approach worship. In other words, quit enjoying worship. True worship can certainly be enjoyable, but it doesn't have to be. True worship transcends my emotions. It may or may not inspire me. And that's okay, because worship is about something else entirely. Something David—the man after God's own heart—knew, something he had, something he experienced and exemplified.

David. The shepherd boy who fought a giant . . . and won. Musician. Poet. Warrior. King. The Bible's portrayal of David is one of its most vivid and inspiring. In fact, the Bible says that God himself referred to David as "a man after my own heart."[157]

A man after God's own heart.

What a distinctive phrase. And a unique status. No one else in Scripture is described that way. And many have tried to guess what it was about David that won him such favor in God's eyes. Was it his faith? His courage? His penitent spirit? Could be. The Bible never tells us. We are left to suppose. So I will: I believe the description of David as "a man after God's own heart" has a lot to do with the way David *worshipped*.

And I suggest to you, if you want to walk in the way of Jesus, if you aspire to be spiritually mature, if you hope to understand and experience what worship is and how it should be done, you can't do much better than to learn from David.

On the Road from Baalah

Well after David had conquered Goliath, he succeeded Saul, the first king of Israel. Soon after, he consolidated his power and once again united the kingdom. He humbled the Philistines, the perennial enemies of the Israelites. He conquered Jerusalem and made it his capital, and then he turned his attention to the Ark of the Covenant.

The ark—the symbol of God's presence with Israel since they came out of Egypt hundreds of years earlier—had been taken as a spoil of battle by the Philistines, Israel's enemies. So once David subdued the

Philistines, he made it a priority to return the ark to its place at the center of Israel's worship life.

So David and "all his men" took off for the town called Baalah of Judah to get the ark. They loaded the ark onto a brand-new cart, one that had never held wheat or hay, goats or sheep, and started the journey toward Jerusalem. Two priests, sons of the high priest, whose names were Uzzah and Ahio, escorted the ark of God as it trundled along in the cart.

It was a party. A parade. Musicians played harps, lyres, cymbals, and tambourines. Dancers whirled and singers sang. People clapped their hands and waved their arms. David laughed and praised God with all his might. Until . . .

The procession hit a rough patch in the road. The oxen pulling the cart stumbled. The cart pitched. The ark started to slide. So Uzzah jumped into action. He grabbed the ark. A moment later, Uzzah lay dead on the ground beside the cart.

The parade stopped. The celebration ceased. Plans changed. Sudden death will do that. The Bible says:

> David was afraid of the LORD that day and said, "How can the ark of the LORD ever come to me?" He was not willing to take the ark of the LORD to be with him in the City of David. Instead, he took it aside to the house of Obed-Edom the Gittite. The ark of the LORD remained in the house of Obed-Edom the Gittite for three months, and the LORD blessed him and his entire household.[158]

Pretty harsh, eh? They just wanted to get the ark from Point A to Point B. They had a plan, they'd bought a brand-new cart, they had their GPS programmed for Baalah of Judah to Jerusalem, and they had the Zion Regional High School Marching Band leading the way.

So what went wrong?

Mark Buchanan, writing in *Christianity Today*, offers an opinion:

Uzzah's willingness to carry the ark on an ox cart [in the first place] was in clear breach of divine command. God had given detailed instruction about how the ark was to be transported: slung on poles and hefted by priests. Freighting the ark on an ox cart was a Philistine notion. It must have seemed to Uzzah— maybe it was even his idea to bring it over from the Philistines— more convenient, efficient, elegant. The latest fashion in worship accoutrements. *Why didn't God think of it? Well, we'll amend that.*[159]

They got ahead of themselves. They had good ideas about worship. They figured they'd do this thing right. I mean, how many times had Uzzah and Ahio led worship, right? They had it down. They knew what would bless the people. They just neglected to consider what would bless *God*.

And the result was disaster. As it sometimes is for us, whether we realize it or not. There is no such thing as prideful worship, self-absorbed worship, or self-satisfied worship. Those terms are self-contradictory.

Humble Yourself

The only true worship is humble worship. Which is why some of us have a hard time feeling like we're "getting through" to God in worship. We feel like our prayers are going nowhere, because we're trying to worship without humbling ourselves. That simply *cannot be done*.

Psalm 51—a psalm of David—says, "The sacrifices of God are a broken spirit; a broken and contrite heart, O God, you will not despise."[160] That is one of the reasons confession is a crucial ingredient of mature worship, because it is the mark of a humble and broken spirit and a contrite heart. It's a part of worship many of us in the church need to rediscover and reclaim, both in private and in public worship.

Many of us think that when we're broken, we can't really worship God. We think that discouragement or depression hobbles us. We're afraid that our sin and suffering disqualifies us. But the opposite is actually true. When you're broken, you're most ready to worship God. When you're bowed down, when you've been knocked to your knees, when you're flat on your face, you're in the perfect posture to worship God, because true worship is humble worship.

Soon after my son became the worship leader for the church my wife and I helped to start, he accompanied a ministry team to a nearby prison for a worship service with the inmates. Afterward he texted me: "It was kinda awesome." I told him that in my experience few people worship more passionately than prisoners and addicts, because unlike too many of us in the church, they come to God with empty hands. They come in brokenness. They come in humility.

I think my son's experience is similar to what the disaster on the road to Jerusalem did for David. If you read further in 2 Samuel 6, you can sense a new tone after the death of Uzzah. A new attitude. A new strategy. And a new focus.

Focus on God's Enjoyment

David was not sure he wanted to mess with the ark again. He'd seen Uzzah turn into a french fry before his very eyes. He wasn't inclined to go back and try it again. But his advisors kept him informed. Three months after the humiliating—and deadly—first attempt to return the ark to Jerusalem, David was told, "The LORD has blessed the household of Obed-Edom and everything he has, because of the ark of God."[161]

So David decided to give it another shot. Only this time would be different. There would still be priests and musicians, singers and worshippers. There would still be clapping and dancing. There would still be a colorful parade. But this time the focus would be different.

Notice what the Bible says: "So David went down and brought up the ark of God from the house of Obed-Edom to the City of David with rejoicing. When those who were carrying the ark of the LORD had taken six steps, he sacrificed a bull and a fattened calf."[162]

Did you miss it? The key detail? The telling difference?

This time, there was no ox cart. The account refers to "those who were carrying the ark." That is, it was slung on poles and hefted by priests, the way God had instructed.

This procession was not styled for the priests' satisfaction or the Levites' convenience or the people's inspiration. The focus this time was on God's enjoyment. It was designed to please him.

True worship is worship that focuses on God. On his enjoyment, not ours. That is why I say: quit enjoying worship. Because your worship—if it is truly worship—should be focused not on what you "get out of it" but on what God gets out of it.

We tend to approach worship as consumers, in which the focus is on *our* experience. Sometimes, even as we claim to be singing for the glory of the risen King, we're actually singing for our own enjoyment and fulfillment. It is as if we're saying to the worship leader, the musicians, the preacher, and the other participants, "Okay, move me! Thrill me! Bless me!" I call it the "Spice Girls" approach to worship: "Give me what I want, what I really, really want."

John Ortberg and Pam Howell, writing in *Leadership Journal*, hit the nail on the head when they say:

> Can you imagine the Israelites, freshly delivered from slavery,
> before a mountain that trembles violently with the presence of

God (Exod. 19), muttering: "We're leaving because we're not singing the songs we like. Like that tambourine song, how come they don't do that tambourine song anymore?"

"I don't like it when Moses leads worship—Aaron's better."

"This is too formal—all that smoke and mystery. I like casual worship."

"It was okay, except for Miriam's dance—too wild, not enough reverence. And I don't like the tambourine."[163]

Scripture doesn't read like that, does it? Why not? Because, "What am *I* getting out of worship?" is the wrong question. The question we ought to be asking is, "What is *God* getting out of my worship?"

As the Westminster Confession puts it, "The chief end of man is to glorify God and enjoy him forever." *Not* the other way around.

But the paradox is this: glorifying God is enjoyable. God-glorifying worship is inspiring and fulfilling. It works that way because worship is the adoration of that which delights us. As C. S. Lewis wrote, "We delight to praise what we enjoy because the praise not merely expresses but completes the enjoyment."[164] In other words, the only personally fulfilling worship is worship that doesn't seek personal fulfillment.

When we take our focus off God and put it toward the style of the service, our own preferences, or even the great skill of the worship team, our worship will become less fulfilling, not more so. This doesn't mean we don't have preferences, nor does it mean that the quality and content of a worship service don't matter; but true worship doesn't require a certain style or a favorite song or anything done according to my preferences. Because *true* worship focuses on God rather than on ourselves and our own desires.

Sacrifice to God

There's yet more evidence that David was focused on God and intent on true worship in that 2 Samuel 6 account. Verse 13 says they had just started the journey when David stopped the procession to make a sacrifice to God.

There was no mention of a sacrifice the first time. That's important. Of course, maybe David's just scared stiff, and who can blame him? The memory of Uzzah's death still had to be fresh in everyone's mind. But I think there's more.

You see, the idea of a sacrifice as God prescribed is not that you give God a bull and a fattened calf and keep the rest; it's that you give God *everything*, you acknowledge that it all belongs to him, and he can do whatever he wants with it. A bull or fattened calf or whatever you sacrifice *represents* the rest. You give God your firstfruits, your best bull, to represent your all.

I think that's what David is doing here. He is intent on making this journey a worship pilgrimage, and sacrifice is central to the worship of the one true God. It had been that way from the beginning.

When Noah and his family exited the ark that had saved them from the Great Flood, he built an altar and sacrificed burnt offerings on it. We're not told that he sang anything or preached anything. The Bible doesn't say there was any liturgical dance or solemn procession. But he sacrificed.

When Abram returned victorious from battle against a confederacy of kings, he met Melchizedek, the king of Jerusalem and "priest of God Most High," and gave him a tithe of all the spoils of battle.[165] He sacrificed.

When Jacob returned to Bethel after wrestling with God and reconciling with his brother Esau, he built a stone pillar there and poured out a drink offering on it. He sacrificed.

And on it goes, throughout Scripture. And so, when David got serious and intent on returning the ark to Jerusalem as an act of worship, he stopped the procession after they had taken only six steps . . . and sacrificed.

Why six steps? I think it was intentional. The seventh step was a Sabbath, like the seventh day of Creation and the seventh day of the week. In fact, some scholars believe the offerings were made *every* seventh step between Baalah of Judah and Jerusalem, which would have required the sacrifice of thousands of bulls and calves.

Either way, David sacrificed. Because true worship is sacrificial. David displayed this attitude again when he approached a man named Araunah the Jebusite about buying his threshing floor for the site of an altar—and the temple David's son and successor would one day build.

Araunah recognized the king, of course, and bowed in front of him with his face to the ground. When David said he intended to buy Araunah's threshing floor, Araunah said, "Let my lord the king take whatever pleases him and offer it up. Here are oxen for the burnt offering, and here are threshing-sledges and ox yokes for the wood. O king, Araunah gives all this to the king."

But David refused. He insisted on paying the man. He said, "I will not sacrifice to the LORD my God burnt offerings that cost me nothing."[166]

Araunah offered the property free of charge. He knew that some kings would simply take it and perhaps even kill the previous owner (as Ahab did later with Naboth[167]). But David would not accept the property as a gift because, he said, "I will not sacrifice to the LORD my God burnt offerings that cost me nothing."

True worship is always costly worship. It will demand something of you. In fact, I would go so far as to say that if you participate in a worship event and have not sacrificed—if it has not been costly to you—then you have not truly and fully worshipped. No matter how "blessed" you may feel, no matter how much the experience "inspired" you, if there was no sacrifice, there was no worship.

That is true not only of our Sunday worship but of our daily worship as well. Giving God two minutes of prayer at breakfast—or even thirty minutes—and then dusting off our hands and doing what we want and going it alone the rest of the day is not worship.

Worship means offering God those two minutes or thirty minutes of prayer at the beginning of that day—or the end, or both—in such a way that it *represents* the rest.

This also means—since true worship is always costly—that the giving of our "tithes and offerings" during a church service is not a "break" or interruption in your worship; it *is* worship! It is perhaps the most worshipful moment in the whole hour. It is a part of the worshipful life that says, "I will not sacrifice to the Lord my God that which costs me nothing."

Engage Mind, Spirit, and Body

Ortberg and Howell, in the article quoted a few pages ago, also say this:

> Some churches specialize in generating emotion. The platform people are expert at moving worshipers to laughter or tears. Attenders gradually learn to evaluate the service in terms of the emotion they feel. . . .
>
> Such worship is often shallow, sometimes artificial, and rarely reflective. Little attention is given to worshiping with the mind. It produces people who have little depth or rootedness. They may develop a "zeal for God, but not according to knowledge" (Rom. 10:2). They become worship junkies, searching for whichever church can supply the best rush.

This is *Scarecrow worship:* it would be better if it only had a brain.

On the other hand, some churches focus keenly on cognitive correctness. They recite great creeds, distribute reams of exegetical information, craft careful prayers ahead of time. And yet the heart and spirit are not seized with the wonder and passion that characterize those in Scripture who must fall on their faces when they encounter the living God. No one is ever so moved that she actually moves. . . .

Those who attend such services may be competent to spot theological error, but the unspoken truth is they're also a little bored. Their worship is dry—it does not connect with their deepest hurts and desires. Rarely does it generate awe or healing, and never raucous joy.

This is *Tin Man worship:* if it only had a heart.[168]

True worship is neither *scarecrow worship* nor *tin man worship*. It is David worship. As the parade approached its destination, the Bible says, "David, wearing a linen ephod, danced before the Lord with all his might, while he and the entire house of Israel brought up the ark of the Lord with shouts and the sound of trumpets.[169]

David leaped and danced before the Lord. He worshipped with body and soul. It was both internal and external, both emotional and physical. But don't miss what follows: "They brought the ark of the Lord and set it in its place inside the tent that David had pitched for it, and David sacrificed burnt offerings and fellowship offerings before the Lord. After he had finished sacrificing the burnt offerings and fellowship offerings, he blessed the people in the name of the Lord Almighty."[170]

His heart was fully engaged, but it never disengaged his mind and his careful awareness of—and obedience to—the Word of the Lord. This may be—at least in part—what Jesus meant when he said, "God is spirit, and his worshipers must worship in *spirit* and in *truth*."[171]

Author and speaker Marva Dawn writes:

> We must avoid the dangers of both intellectualism and of emotionalism. To focus on the mind alone won't engage people's will and heart so that they act on what they know. To focus exclusively on training the emotions encourages faith without substance. Genuine worship corrects both extremes, for in it, as Welton Gaddy affirms, "God is to be loved and honored by all of one's being."[172]

In fact, that last phrase, "all of one's being," ought to refer not only to heart and mind, but also to our physical bodies. I think it's healthy to bow during worship, to lift your hands as a way of reaching out to God, to cup your hands to indicate your prayer for God's filling or his blessing, or even to kneel or dance or pump your fists in the air. At the *heart* of worship is a willingness to love God with your whole heart, mind, soul, and strength—an abandonment to worship with emotion, intellect, spirit, and body.

Step Out of Your Comfort Zone

A curious detail appears in the account of the ark's return to Jerusalem. When David danced before the ark on its journey, the Bible describes his apparel: "David, wearing a linen ephod, danced before the LORD with all his might, while he and the entire house of Israel brought up the ark of the LORD with shouts and the sound of trumpets."[173]

David's name was mentioned six times already in that passage, and not once did the writer mention what he was wearing. In fact, this verse may be the only time in the whole Bible that we're told what David wore.

Why is that?

I think it is because it was significant that he wore not his elaborate, ornate royal robes but the humbler, simpler, next-to-nothing linen ephod.

The Bible doesn't tell us where and when he doffed his kingly robes down to the cheap duds, but he did it. And he did it before he danced.

He may have done it for comfort. It would have been much easier to dance in an ephod than in his kingly apparel.

He may have done it for humility's sake. It may have been a statement that he danced not as a king but as a man, as a child, as a humble servant of God.

Or he may have done it for another reason. Or for all of these combined. He may have danced in his linen garment to shed all inhibitions and get out of his comfort zone. And I think in that seldom-noticed detail is a lesson.

Most of us hold back from true worship, from wholehearted worship. We have our fears, our inhibitions, our reservations. It may be pride. It may be the fear of what people might say. Our doubts. Sensitivity to a spouse. Insecurity.

Guess what? None of it is worth it. Nothing is important enough to stand in the way when God invites you to dance. Nothing.

That is clearly how David felt. When his own wife, Michal, berated him after the fact for what she considered conduct unbecoming a king, he answered, "It was before the LORD, who chose me rather than your father or anyone from his house when he appointed me ruler over the LORD's people Israel—I will celebrate before the LORD. I will become even more undignified than this, and I will be humiliated in my own eyes."[174]

True worship will change you. It will move you. It will bless you. But it might also scare you.

Why? Because, as Annie Dillard has written, every week when we gather to worship, we are like "children playing on the floor with their chemistry sets, mixing up a batch of TNT to kill a Sunday morning." In fact, she adds, "It is madness to wear ladies' straw hats and velvet hats to church; we should all be wearing crash helmets."[175]

True worship is costly—and dangerous. It is an encounter with an awesome, infinite, almighty God who fills us with wonder, trembling, hope, and fear.

To quote Marva Dawn again, "Everything that we do in worship should *kill* us, but especially the parts of the service in which we hear the Word—the Scripture lessons and the sermon."[176]

Worship should kill us—our sin, self-centeredness, self-absorption, self-sufficiency, and self-satisfaction. It ought to crucify us, challenge us, convict us, and change us. I would even go so far as to say that if your worship is comfortable, it is "cowardly lion worship"—that is, worship that is afraid to risk. If your worship isn't costing you, if it doesn't stretch you, if it doesn't scare you, if it's not *at least a little bit* out of your comfort zone, then you're probably not worshipping.

But if, on the other hand, you leave worship a little breathless, maybe trembling, maybe thinking you sang too loud, or gave too much, or made a fool of yourself, or got too close to the flame of the holy, living God, then maybe you have experienced a little of what the writer to the Hebrews meant when he wrote:

> You have not come to a mountain that can be touched. . . . But you have come to Mount Zion, to the heavenly Jerusalem, the city of the living God. You have come to thousands upon thousands of angels in joyful assembly, to the church of the first-born, whose names are written in heaven. You have come to

God, the judge of all men, to the spirits of righteous men made perfect, to Jesus the mediator of a new covenant, and to the sprinkled blood.[177]

If your eyebrows are singed in worship, if you feel like you're playing with TNT, if you're out of your comfort zone, then you may be smack dab at the heart of worship, which the same writer to the Hebrews referred to as worshipping God acceptably.

Author Richard Caemmerer told of a churchgoer greeting the pastor at the door after a worship service. "Pastor," the churchgoer said, "that was a wonderful service."

The pastor smiled and said, "That remains to be seen."[178]

~~§~~ *Prayer*

Almighty God, you are infinitely worthy to receive glory and honor and power and praise.

Forgive me for ever having sought my own enjoyment in worship.

Humble me, Lord.

Transform me.

Let me never offer worship to you that costs me nothing.

Teach me to worship with mind, soul, heart, and strength.

Break down my walls,

and help me to worship you with wild abandon,

surrendering and escaping my comfort zones,

and finding blessing in blessing you with my worship,

in Jesus' name. Amen.

CHAPTER TWELVE

Quit Living in the Center
of God's Will

We use a lot of thoughtless, unexamined terms
and phrases in the church and in Christian families.

For example, as I mentioned in Chapter Two, we talk about "blessing our food," a phrase we use to refer to saying "grace," the prayers we offer before eating a meal. Chances are, we get that terminology from (among other places) the story of Jesus feeding a crowd of five thousand, which says he took "the five loaves and the two fish . . . looked up to heaven and said a blessing."[179] However, we can be confident that the blessing he said was not "Bless us, O Lord, and these thy gifts which we are about to receive from thy bounty," but "Blessed art thou, O Lord our God, King of the universe, who brings forth bread from the earth," and "Blessed art thou, O Lord our God, King of the universe, who creates various kinds of food." In other words, Jesus didn't bless the *food*; he blessed the *Father* and gave thanks for the food.

Have you ever responded to someone who asked you to do something by saying, "Let me pray about it, and I'll get back to you"? While I'm sure there are exceptions, for many of us, "Let me pray about it" is Christian code for "I don't want to, but it'll be easier to say no after a little time has passed." Saying "Let me pray about it" takes the pressure off of me and kinda puts the blame on God, a scenario that usually leads to another code phrase: "I don't feel led."

Or, to use another example, we sometimes pray for "traveling mercies." That means we're going on a trip and we want God to protect us. Jon Acuff, on his hilarious *Stuff Christians Like* blog (which inspired his book by the same name), plumbs the immense depths of this terminology when he writes:

> The first time my brother prayed for "traveling mercies" I thought he was praying for a band. Honestly, it sounds like a side project Dave Matthews and that insanely muscular violin player are involved in. "Tonight, opening up for Widespread Panic, it's the Traveling Mercies!"
>
> Apparently though, traveling mercies are not a hemp-loving band but rather a prayer request to have a good trip. A safe trip, a happy trip, a fun trip, etc. But what exactly are traveling mercies? Have you ever stopped to think about what we're asking God for? I did and came up with a short list of what I think traveling mercies are when you're on a road trip:
>
> 1. That you will hear Tom Cochrane's song, "Life is a Highway" at least once.

2. That you and your father-in law will not get kicked off the New Jersey turnpike because your moving van weighs too much.

3. That you will not bust capillaries in your eyeballs from drinking too many Diet Rockstars or other energy drinks.

4. That you will employ ninja-like focus in not having to use the bathroom at a gas station.

5. That if your ninja-like focus breaks down you will employ a hover move so that you don't touch any surface (the floor, the door handle, the toilet, etc.) within the gas station bathroom.

6. That your friend Carsten will not throw up in the car when you drive past a paper mill.

7. That you will not throw your flat tire with rim still attached over the siderail in the mountains of North Carolina because you are dumb and in college and named Jon Acuff.

8. That none of your friends will tell you stories that start off with, "let me tell you about this weird dream I had last night . . ."

9. That you will honor the "eat at least one piece of beef jerky while on a road trip" rule. Unless you're vegan.

10. That you will not be wooed by siren gas stations that appear close to the highway but upon getting off to get gas turn out to be 19 miles away.[180]

I'm not sure I pray all that when I pray before a trip, but I *have* gotten more specific in my praying at such times. The Bible says, "You do not have because you do not ask,"[181] so when I prepare to travel, I ask—for safety, for protection from germs, for cooperative flight schedules or traffic patterns, and so on. Maybe for some people "traveling mercies" covers all that. But I'd rather know for sure what I'm saying, especially when I pray.

Still, "blessing our food," "let me pray about it," and "traveling mercies" are just the beginning. We use a countless number and variety of expressions without really reflecting on what we're saying. Depending on our background or denominational leanings, we might refer to "a word," "word of wisdom," or "word from the Lord." "Trophies of grace." "Unspoken request." "Prepare our hearts for prayer." "Getting in the Word." "Have a burden for." "Lift you up in prayer." "Pray through." "My walk." "Getting on our faces." "Standing under the spout where the glory comes out."

Much of the time, I guess we know what we mean, even if others may not. And maybe some of the phrases we use are a form of shorthand that expresses something so well that it's hard to say the same thing in another way. But such phrases also tend to cloud the issue and confuse rather than clarify.

I think "living in the center of God's will" is one of those phrases.

Pardon Me, Sir, Where Is the Center of God's Will?

What does that mean? Where *is* the center of God's will? Susanna Wesley (the mother of Charles and John) wrote:

> In the center of His Will, we find direction and guidance;
> for He knows the Way.
> In the center of His Will, we have His protection and
> provision;
> for He is our refuge.

At the center of His Will, we have assurance of hope, fullness
of joy, and the promise of peace with us;
for HE is with us!![182]

Nice sentiments. But where is it? How do I find it? How do I know when
I'm there? How do I stay there? Is the will of God like a circle that follows me everywhere I go, and sometimes I veer too close to one side or
the other? Is it like a ten by twelve room with invisible walls, and I have
to stay close to one spot or I might leave the room without realizing it?
Vague sentiments are nice, but I need some answers.

Steve McVey writes:

> Multitudes of sermons have been preached through the years
> giving the roadmap for finding the will of God. The problem is
> that when we follow those religious maps, we discover that they
> only lead to uncertainty and frustration.
>
> I have met countless people who have nearly driven them-
> selves to desperation trying to find the perfect answer about
> God's will for their lives. Many Christians live in almost neurotic
> fear that they have missed it (or will miss it in the future). They
> live in terrible self-doubt about past choices, racking their brains
> in self-analysis: "Did I marry the right person? Did I marry the
> wrong person? Did I go to the right college? Did I go into the
> right profession? Am I working at the right company? Living in
> the right town?" They are paralyzed in their present decision-
> making in the same kind of self-doubt.[183]

I agree. I've witnessed the same thing. All conscientious followers of Jesus
want to fulfill God's will. But the idea of living in the "center" of God's
will is not a biblical concept. McVey says, "Nowhere does the Scripture

tell us that the will of God is something that we have to find."[184] It's just not there. Honest. Go ahead, get your Bible. Look it up. See if you can find a passage that says we must find God's will or make sure we live in the center of his will. I'll wait.

Back so soon? Didn't find it, did you? I thought so.

If you really looked, you would find that the Bible does talk about the will of God. It tells us point-blank that God's will is for us to give thanks.[185] It says that God's will is for us to be sanctified.[186] We are told not to be conformed to this world and its ways, but to be transformed by the renewing of our minds, so that we can experience his good, perfect, and pleasing will for us.[187] But nowhere are we urged to search for God's will or agonize over the particulars of God's will. And neither are we told to live in the center of God's will.

So let's quit. Just cut it out. Quit "living in the center of God's will." And start boldly embracing uncertainty instead.

Uncertainty Is So . . . Uncertain

We live in uncertain times. The economy is uncertain. Jobs are seldom secure these days. Conventional wisdom keeps changing. And for many of us, it gets real personal. We want to believe God will answer our prayers *the way we want him to,* but what if he has different plans? We want him to heal us, we want him to fix our family, we want him to save our job, but what if he has a different agenda? And what if we don't much like his agenda?

One of the hardest things about the life of faith is, well, that it takes faith. The ancient Israelites were actually expected to sacrifice their first-born lamb from each ewe—that is, *before* they knew any other lambs were going to be born. Peter had to step out of the boat when he'd never walked on water before. We're asked to follow without knowing where the path will lead.

I hate that.

You probably do, too.

It's all so uncertain. And most of us don't like uncertainty. We want sure things. We require safety and surety. We think something's wrong, someone's at fault, if there's no guarantee. We want wealth without risk, truth without consequences, gain without pain.

But that's not how God works. That's not how *faith* works.

A Michmash Is Different from a Hodgepodge

Jonathan was the son of King Saul. Though his appearance on the biblical stage is brief, he is one of the great characters in the grand drama of Scripture.

Though he was heir to the throne of Israel and a great warrior in his own right, Jonathan loved David, whom the prophet Samuel had anointed to succeed Saul. On one occasion, Jonathan camped with his father and the armies of Israel near a little town called Gibeah.

Though Saul was king and had all the political power necessary to wage war against Philistia, the arch enemies of God's people, he didn't. He marched the army into the field. He set up an encampment near the Philistine outpost at Michmash. But instead of acting, the Bible says, "Saul was staying on the outskirts of Gibeah under a pomegranate tree in Migron. With him were about six hundred men."[188]

Saul was immobile. Going nowhere. He had a mere six hundred men and a severe weapons shortage: only Saul and Jonathan had swords. The rest of the army had stakes or farming implements. They were an army without arms.

So Saul waited under a pomegranate tree, because from his perspective success was pretty unlikely. He faced an opportunity, he sat at a crucial crossroads, but he froze.

But not Jonathan.

Have you ever wondered why some people just seem to fearlessly step into divine moments? Some people seem to swim in the stream of God's power and turn everything they touch into a miracle, as if the tips of their fingers have a kind of "God dust" on them. They have the same opportunities you and I have, but they respond to those moments differently.

I think we see that difference at work in the story of Jonathan at Gibeah, and I believe the difference is faith—a certain kind of faith. A faith that is not afraid of risk and uncertainty, and even embraces those things.

Know What You Don't Know

King Saul, like many modern Christians who live in neurotic fear of missing God's will, was afraid to make a decision. He preferred to wait. To sit. And it's hard to blame him, really. He had two swords in the whole army. The Philistines had every advantage: numbers, weaponry, field position, you name it. Holding off was probably the smart move.

But Jonathan was not content to sit under a pomegranate tree. He said to his young armor-bearer, "Come, let's go over to the outpost of those uncircumcised fellows. Perhaps the LORD will act on our behalf."[189]

Stop.

Did you catch something strange there?

Jonathan said, "*Perhaps* the LORD will act on our behalf."

Perhaps.

Perhaps?

This is not how we usually hear people talk about God and his will, is it? Truthfully, have you ever heard anyone say such a thing in your church? And we certainly don't expect such a phrase from people in the Bible.

We expect Jonathan—a man of faith, a hero of the Bible, a "braveheart" if there ever was one—to say, "And God *will* act on our behalf! I've prayed about it. It's God's will. How can we lose?" Right? If God is for us, who can be against us?

But he didn't say that. He said, "Let's go over to the Philistine camp and pick a fight with those pagans. *Maybe* God will help us."

Well, yippee. Woo. Hoo.

Does that inspire you? Maybe? Perhaps? Hope so?

I think one of the things you find in people of great faith is this: they know what they don't know. And that doesn't scare them. They're okay with that.

Pastor and author Erwin McManus, in a sermon that partly inspired this chapter (and also inspired his book *Seizing Your Divine Moment*), says this:

> As I interview people about God's will for their life, you know what I find? Most people know exactly what they're supposed to do. But what they pray about is not God's will but how to change the outcome or the consequences of God's will. Most of the time, when we're trying to process God's will what we're trying to do is find out how to eliminate all the pain and suffering involved on the journey.[190]

Exactly. That's why we tend to obsess about every little detail of "finding God's will" and "living in the center of God's will." We're hoping to eliminate uncertainty and danger. But Jonathan had clearly come to terms with the fact that he didn't *know* God would bless his action.

In his award-winning book, *An Unstoppable Force*, McManus writes:

> You've heard it said that the safest place to be is in the center of God's will. I am sure this promise was well intended, but it is neither true nor innocuous. . . . The truth of the matter is that the center of God's will is not a safe place but the most dangerous place in the world! God fears nothing and no one! God moves with intentionality and power. To live outside of God's will puts us in danger; to live in his will makes us dangerous.[191]

So it's okay not to know what's going to happen next. It's okay not to know exactly what God is going to do. It's okay sometimes to take a risk and say, "*Perhaps* God. . . ."

That's not the end of the faith process, but it's a crucial beginning. Christians and churches in general suffer from a surfeit of so-called certainty, a neurotic need to control people and events, a faithless addiction to believing we know what we're doing. But most of the time, if we are honest, we don't know.

Know What You *Do* Know

Far too many of us are afraid to take a step unless we're convinced God wills it and will bless it. But Jonathan was willing to risk his life on the *chance* that God might use him.

He was either a man of faith or he was totally insane. Often those two things look pretty much the same, anyway.

But after Jonathan said, "Perhaps the LORD will act on our behalf," he said something equally important. He said, "Nothing can hinder the LORD from saving, whether by many or by few."[192]

Jonathan was willing to risk his life on the *chance* that God might use him, but he had more to go on than a feeling, a sensation, a tentative possibility. He knew God. He knew God's ways. He knew that nothing can hinder the Lord from saving, whether by many or by few.

He knew what he *didn't* know. But he also knew what he *did* know.

He didn't know for sure if God would grant him victory, but he did know that God would save his people. He didn't know if God would work through him and his armor-bearer, but he knew that God would work. And he was willing to lay down his life based on the thing he didn't know *and* the thing he did know.

That is a faith God will honor.

I may not know in detail what God's plans are for me, but I know that nothing can hinder him from saving, one way or another. I don't know if I give away my firstfruits that I'll have money for my Mastercard bill—especially since God didn't authorize most of the charges on that bill—but I do know that he will find a way to honor those who honor him in their finances. I don't know if God is going to heal the people I'm praying for, but I do know that he wants me to be faithful—and faith-filled—in prayer.

You may not know if you're in the center of God's will, whatever that means. There may be a lot of things you don't know. But there are also some things you do know: things about God, his ways, his promises. What are they? Remind yourself of them. List them. Repeat them until they're embedded in your mind and heart. Know what you know.

Go Until God Says No

I really have to feel for Jonathan's young armor-bearer. It was his job to protect the prince. To serve him. To carry Jonathan's armor. To make sure he had the armor, weapons, and care he needed before, during, and after a battle. But remember, only Saul and Jonathan had swords. The armor-bearer didn't.

But when Jonathan proposed a commando raid on the enemy's camp, just the two of them, the armor-bearer said, "Do all that you have in mind. . . . Go ahead; I am with you heart and soul."[193]

Two thumbs up. Really? I gotta say, I don't think I would have responded that way. Remember, the armor-bearer got to carry the armor. That's how he got his job title. He carried Jonathan's armor. He didn't wear it. He carried it. I think if I were him, I would have said, "Beggin' your pardon, sir, but since you're not *sure* how this is going to turn out, how about *I* wear the armor this time?"

But he didn't say that. Gotta give him credit. He said, "Do it! I'm with you!" And that's when Jonathan revealed his strategy. His super-secret plan:

> Jonathan said, "Come, then; we will cross over towards the men and let them see us. If they say to us, 'Wait there until we come to you,' we will stay where we are and not go up to them. But if they say, 'Come up to us,' we will climb up, because that will be our sign that the LORD has given them into our hands."[194]

This may not have been the worst military strategy of all time, but I'm guessing it's not heavily studied at military academies today. Jonathan suggested they begin the battle by announcing their presence and revealing their position. Brilliant.

If it were me, I think I would have said, "Okay, here's the deal. We sneak up on 'em. In the dark. Wearing dresses. We kill 'em as quietly as we can, and if they wake up, we scream like little girls and say, 'They went thataway!'"

But Jonathan chose a different strategy, because he's not doing this based on human intellect. He's in a moment of God's choosing.

His plan was to step into the pass over which the Philistine outpost loomed, let the enemy see him, and put the rest in God's hands.

Has God ever called you to do something so dramatic, so terrifying to you, so outside your comfort zone, that you knew if you did it you could not guarantee—or even guess—the results? McManus says: "There's this interesting framework in men and women that God uses to change history. They have an advance mentality. They go unless they get a no."[195]

That seems to have been both Jonathan's and his armor-bearer's attitude:

> So both of them showed themselves to the Philistine outpost. "Look!" said the Philistines. "The Hebrews are crawling out of the holes they were hiding in." The men of the outpost shouted to Jonathan and his armor-bearer, "Come up to us and we'll teach you a lesson." So Jonathan said to his armor-bearer, "Climb up after me; the LORD has given them into the hand of Israel."[196]

Again, I can't believe the armor-bearer would not be saying, "Come again? Say *what*?" I mean, they've alerted the enemy—who, by the way, have no shortage of weapons—Jonathan's climbing a cliff, the Philistines are just waiting on top, saying, "Climb that sheer cliff, pull yourself over the ledge, take your time standing up, and we'll teach you a lesson!"

And Jonathan says, "Ooh, this is good. We've got 'em right where we want 'em."

Are you kidding me?

Can Jonathan really be thinking things through? Has he thought ahead to the point when he and his armor-bearer have climbed to the very top of the cliff, their hands are raw, and they have to pull themselves up over the edge, scramble to their feet, draw their one sword, and engage the Philistines who—oh, wait a minute. Maybe the Philistines wouldn't let them get that far. Maybe the enemy—to whom they had announced themselves—would attack when Jonathan and his armor-bearer were at the most vulnerable point in their climb. But Jonathan doesn't seem to be thinking about all that. He is apparently thinking more along the lines of, "Man, they won't know what hit 'em!"

Then again, maybe I'm not giving him enough credit. Maybe he figured, "If God hasn't stopped me by then, I'll either win a miraculous battle or die in a blaze of glory. Either way, nothing can hinder God from saving, whether by many or by few."

It is truly amazing to me that Jonathan wasted no time agonizing over whether God's will was this or that. I think it's even significant that he didn't choose the easy way. He could have told his armor-bearer—it certainly would've made more sense—"If they say to us, 'Climb on up and walk right into our trap,' we will stay where we are and not go up to them."

That's what I would have said. Jonathan and his man are at the *bottom* of the cliff. It makes much more sense to say, "We want the Philistines to climb down that cliff face, so we can just whack off their legs before they hit the ground. *That* will be our sign that the Lord has given them into our hands."

But Jonathan said the exact opposite. He knew God could make the Philistines say anything he wanted them to say. And he knew if God wanted to say no, if God wanted to turn him back, he could make the Philistines say, "Go away, or I shall taunt you a second time!"

Not a Monty Python fan? Okay, never mind, then.

But Jonathan figured he'd go until he got a no:

Jonathan climbed up, using his hands and feet, with his armor-bearer right behind him. The Philistines fell before Jonathan, and his armor-bearer followed and killed behind him.

In that first attack Jonathan and his armor-bearer killed some twenty men in an area of about half an acre. Then panic struck the whole army—those in the camp and field, and those in the outposts and raiding parties—and the ground shook. It was a panic sent by God.[197]

What a contrast his behavior was to that of many Christians today. We fret and obsess and live in fear (which is demonstrably not God's will for us, according to 2 Timothy 1:7) instead of stepping out in courageous faith, believing that God is big enough to save, whether by many or by few. Jonathan knew that, three thousand years ago. He knew what he didn't know, he knew what he did know, and he went—boldly embracing uncertainty—until God said "no." And God not only blessed his efforts, but he took over and fought the rest of the battle for him.

Take a Relaxative and Call Me in the Morning

Look, I'm probably the worst at wanting control and wanting to know ahead of time what's going to happen next. But I know this: I know *nothing* next to what God knows. And I know that God loves me, he loves you, he loves the church, he loves the world. I know his plans for all of us are good. I know his power is unlimited. And so, step by step, moment by moment, I'm willing to trust him and do my best to live in the freedom Steve McVey urges:

> It's not up to you to keep yourself in the center of God's will. It's God's responsibility to do that. That's why it's called grace.

And He will do exactly that. Don't worry that you'll get out of the will of God. He'll take care of things.

God has a calling (a plan) for you, and He will ensure that you know it and do it. The Bible says that He is faithful not only to make His calling known to you, but also to bring it to pass in your life (see 1 Thessalonians 5:24).

So don't accept the lie that you have to find God's will. It isn't necessary for you to take on such pressure. You weren't intended to carry that responsibility. That's His role. What is our response to be? "In everything give thanks; for *this is God's will for you* in Christ Jesus" (1 Thessalonians 5:18). Just relax, yield yourself to Him, and know He'll make it happen in His time and in His way. The only thing left for us to do is to say, "Thank You!" *That* is his will for you.[198]

~~§§~~ *Prayer*

Lord God Adonai, there is so much I don't know.

I know nothing next to what you know.

I don't know what my future holds.

I don't even know what tomorrow—or the next five minutes—holds.

But I know that you love me.

I know that you love the church.

I know that you love the world.

I know your plans for me are good.

I know your power is unlimited and your love is unconditional.

And so, step by step, and moment by moment,

    help me to trust you,

to be courageous and full of faith,
to boldly embrace uncertainty,
and to rely on you for whatever results,
in Jesus' name. Amen.

A Final Word

Thank you for reading this book. I hope it has challenged you. I have prayed that it will change you and how you relate to God, his people, and his world. I mean that; I have prayed for you. I have prayed for everyone who reads this book. I have prayed fervently and specifically:

I pray for you to quit going to church . . . and start being the church.

I pray you will quit saying your prayers . . . and make it a habit instead to keep company with God.

I pray for you to quit reading the Bible, using it instead as a means of relating to him.

I pray you will quit sharing your faith . . . and share your life.

I pray for you to quit tithing and replace the "ten percent way" of the law with the "hundred percent way" of Jesus.

I pray that you will quit volunteering . . . and start exercising your gifts with greater effectiveness and enjoyment in God's service.

I pray that you will quit being nice . . . and be real instead.

I pray for you to quit helping the poor . . . and unite with them instead.

I pray for you to quit fellowshipping and start partying.

I pray that you will give up all attempts to be good and instead focus on one thing—the better thing—of daily dwelling in Jesus' presence.

I pray that you will quit enjoying worship and inspiring yourself in worship . . . and instead focus your worship on making God happy.

And, finally, I pray that you will quit camping out in the center of God's will and instead be courageous and full of faith, boldly embracing uncertainty and trusting God for the results.

I pray other things for you, too. I pray for you to prosper and be in health, even as your soul prospers.[199] I pray that God will overflow your life.[200] I pray that you will be fruitful, grow spiritually, and become mighty for God and his kingdom.[201] I pray that you will recommend this book to others and help extend its message and ministry. I pray that you will give away copies of this book to anyone you think might be helped by it. And I pray that you will let me know, via my website www.bobhostetler.com, if it has made a difference in your life.

Thanks again for reading.

NOTES

Introduction

1. George MacDonald, *The Curate's Awakening* (Minneapolis: Bethany House Publishers, 1985), 23.
2. Matthew 26:30; Mark 14:26.
3. Acts 17:28.
4. Jude 1:3.
5. Michael Spencer, *Mere Churchianity* (Colorado Springs, CO: Waterbrook Press, 2010), 50, 54.

Chapter One

6. Acts 2:41–47.
7. Tim Stafford, *Surprised by Jesus* (Downers Grove, IL: InterVarsity Press, 2006), 31.
8. I am indebted to Brian McLaren for the linkage between the Nicene Creed and what it means to be the church, and for the outline of the thoughts that follow in this chapter.
9. Acts 2:42.
10. 2 Corinthians 3:18b.
11. Leonard S. Kravitz, *Pirke Avot: A Modern Commentary on Jewish Ethics* (New York: UAHC Press, 1993), 4.
12. Stafford, *Surprised*, 99–100.
13. Acts 2:41–46.
14. Brian McLaren, *A New Kind of Christian* (San Francisco: Jossey-Bass, 2001).
15. Steve Fee, "Madly," EMI Christian Music Publishing, 2002, worshiptogether.com.
16. Acts 2:41–47.
17. McLaren, *A New Kind*, 156.

Chapter Two

18. Luke 11:1.
19. Revelation 3:20.
20. Brennan Manning, *The Ragamuffin Gospel* (Sisters, OR: Multnomah Publishers, 2005), 59.
21. Luke 19:1–10 (BQP: Bob's Questionable Paraphrase).
22. Philip Yancey, *Prayer* (Grand Rapids, MI: Zondervan, 2006), 62.
23. Genesis 18.
24. Psalm 6:3; Psalm 13:1–2; Psalm 35:17; Psalm 79:5; and so on.

25. 2 Samuel 2:1.

26. Genesis 32.

27. 1 Thessalonians 5:17 NASB.

28. Anthony Bloom, *Beginning to Pray* (Mahwah, NJ: Paulist Press, 1970), 88–89.

29. Brennan Manning, *Abba's Child* (Colorado Springs, CO: NavPress, 2002), 124–125.

30. Revelation 3:20.

Chapter Three

31. Michael Rovin, "God's Ten Suggestions," *Weekly World News*, February 12, 2007, 11.

32. Dick Siegel, "God Speaks to Tourist Through Burning Bush," *Weekly World News*, February 12, 2007, 27.

33. "Headlines From Tomorrow," *Weekly World News*, February 12, 2007, 8–9.

34. Exodus 33:12–13.

35. Eugene Peterson, *The Invitation: A Simple Guide to the Bible* (Colorado Springs, CO: NavPress, 2008), 13.

36. Exodus 33:13–14.

37. Jeremiah 15:16 NJB.

38. Exodus 33:15–16.

39. Exodus 33:17–18.

40. 2 Peter 3:9 NLT.

41. Matthew 5:4.

42. Exodus 33:18.

43. Exodus 33:21–23.

44. Lyrics to "He Hideth My Soul" by Fanny J. Crosby, hymn, published 1890.

Chapter Four

45. John 1:14.

46. John 1:14 *The Message*.

47. Mike Erre, *The Jesus of Suburbia* (Nashville, TN: W Publishing Group, 2006), 181. Emphasis added.

48. 1 Thessalonians 1:4–8, 2:5–8, *The Message*.

49. 1 Thessalonians 2:8.

50. Matthew 5:13.

51. 2 Corinthians 5:20, *New Living Translation* (1996).

52. Erre, *The Jesus of Suburbia*, 181–182.

53. Acts 8:1 ESV.

54. Steve McVey, *52 Lies Heard in Church Every Sunday* (Eugene, OR: Harvest House Publishers, 2011), 105–106.

55. Matthew 10:8.

56. Rob Bell, *Velvet Elvis* (Grand Rapids, MI: Zondervan, 2005), 167.

57. Matthew 10:11.

Chapter Five

58. Robert Wuthnow, "Pious Materialism: How Americans View Faith and Money," *The Christian Century* (March 3, 1993): 239–242.

59. Leviticus 27:30, 32–33.

60. Matthew 22:21.

61. Luke 14:33 NLT.

62. Luke 21:1–4.

63. Luke 18:22.

64. Andy Stanley, *Enemies of the Heart* (Colorado Springs, CO: Multnomah Books, 2011), 155–156.

65. Galatians 3:24–25 KJV.

66. Acts 2:44–45.

67. Acts 4:32.

68. Matthew 10:8.

69. 2 Corinthians 9:7.

70. 2 Corinthians 9:6, 8–11.

71. 2 Corinthians 9:11a, emphasis added.

72. Genesis 22:17–18a.

73. Matthew 5:16.

74. 2 Corinthians 8:1–3.

75. Matthew 10:8; James 1:17.

Chapter Six

76. Acts 6:1–7 NCV.

77. Acts 6:2 *The Message.*

78. Acts 7:1–8:2.

79. Romans 12:6–8 GW.

80. 1 Corinthians 12:1.

81. 1 Corinthians 12:4–6.

82. Charles Swindoll, *Growing Deep in the Christian Life* (Grand Rapids: Zondervan Publishers, 1995), 422.

83. 1 Corinthians 12:8–10.

84. Romans 12:6–8; 1 Corinthians 12:8–10; Ephesians 4:11.

85. 1 Corinthians 12:11.

86. 1 Corinthians 12:12–13.

87. 1 Corinthians 12:14–20.

88. 1 Corinthians 12:21–27.

89. John 13:1–17.

Chapter Seven

90. Paul Coughlin, *No More Christian Nice Guy* (Bloomington, MI: Bethany House Publishers, 2005), 14, 15–16.

91. Zechariah 9:9.

92. Psalm 69:9.

93. Peter Marshall, *A Man Called Peter* (Grand Rapids, MI: Chosen Books, 1951), 312–313.

94. John 2:15a.

95. C. S. Lewis, *The Lion, the Witch, and the Wardrobe* (New York: HarperCollins Publishers, 1994), 78–80.

96. Revelation 19:11–16.

97. John 2:17.

98. 1 Corinthians 6:19a.

99. William Shakespeare, *Julius Caesar*, act 1, scene 2, lines 140–141.

100. Margery Williams Bianco and Gennadii Spirin, *The Velveteen Rabbit: Or How Toys Become Real* (Tarrytown, NY: Marshall Cavendish Corporation, 2011), 12.

101. Genesis 3:10.

102. Coughlin, *No More*, 45.

103. 1 John 4:18.

104. James 5:16.

105. William Shakespeare, *King Lear*, act 5, scene 3, line 323.

106. John Johnson, "Quit Being Nice," sermon transcript, Oxford, Ohio, February 25, 2007.

107. Matthew 5:23–24, 18:15–17.

108. Ephesians 4:26 HCSB.

109. Coughlin, *No More*, 45–46.

110. Matthew 5:33, 37a *The Message*.

111. John 11:1–16.

112. Mark 1:35–38.

113. Luke 10:38–42.

114. Henry Cloud and John Townsend, *Boundaries* (Grand Rapids: Zondervan, 1992), 36.

Chapter Eight

115. Thanks to Major Bill Bender (the younger) for helping with some of these memories of Fifi.

116. John 12:1–8.

117. Deuteronomy 15:10–11 *The Message*.

118. Mark 12:41–44.

119. John 4:18.

120. Luke 13:12; Luke 19:5; John 4:7; John 5:6.

121. Matthew 8:20.

122. Matthew 17:24–27.

123. John 1:38–39.

124. Luke 19:28–40.

125. Mark 14:13–15.

126. John 19:38–42.

127. John 12:8a.

128. Shane Claiborne, *The Irresistible Revolution* (Grand Rapids: Zondervan, 2006), 63.

129. Peter J. Leithart, "Torah and Social Justice," *First Things*, web article, July 29, 2011, www.firstthings.com/onthesquare/2011/07/torah-and-social-justice. Bold type in original.

130. Matthew 6:3–4.

131. Rob Bell, *Velvet Elvis* (Grand Rapids: Zondervan, 2005), 168.

132. Acts 3:1–11 NLT.

133. Michael Spencer, *Mere Churchianity* (Colorado Springs: Waterbrook Press, 2010), 205.

134. 2 Corinthians 8:9.

Chapter Nine

135. Clement of Alexandria, *Paedogogus*, Book 3, Chapter 11.

136. This is a reasonable assumption based on Mary's inside knowledge of the wine shortage in John 2:3, which would have been a closely guarded secret within the groom's family.

137. John 2:11 ESV.

138. Matthew 9:10–11.

139. Matthew 11:19.

140. Luke 14:15–24.

141. Acts 2:13 ISV.

142. Acts 2:11.

143. Acts 2:42a.

144. Tony Campolo, "The Kingdom of God Is a Party!" sermon delivered to the Crystal Cathedral and aired on the Hour of Power, September 27, 2009, www.tonycampolo.org/doc/crystalcathedral/The_Kingdom_of_God.pdf. Used by permission.

145. Rob Bell, *Velvet Elvis* (Grand Rapids: Zondervan, 2005), 170.

146. Luke 14:21b.

Chapter Ten

147. Romans 7:18–20 *The Message*.

148. Steve McVey, *52 Lies Heard in Church Every Sunday* (Eugene, OR: Harvest House Publishers, 2011), 62.

149. Galatians 5:16–25, 6:7–8.

150. Galatians 3:10a.

151. Galatians 3:10–14.

152. John 4:5–15.

153. John 4:28–30.

154. Luke 19:5–10.

155. Luke 8:1–2.

156. Luke 10:41–42.

Chapter Eleven

157. 1 Samuel 13:14; Acts 13:22.

158. 2 Samuel 6:1–11.

159. Mark Buchanan, "Dance of the God-Struck," *Christianity Today*, October 7, 2002.

160. Psalm 51:17.

161. 2 Samuel 6:12a.

162. 2 Samuel 6:12b–13.

163. John Ortberg and Pam Howell, "Can You Engage Both Heart and Mind?" *Leadership Journal*, Spring 1999.

164. C. S. Lewis, *Reflections on the Psalms* (New York: Harcourt, Brace & World, 1958), 94–95.

165. Genesis 14:18b.

166. 2 Samuel 24:18–25.

167. 1 Kings 21.

168. Ortberg and Howell, "Can You Engage."

169. 2 Samuel 6:14–15.

170. 2 Samuel 6:17–18.

171. John 4:24, emphasis added.

172. Marva Dawn, *Reaching Out Without Dumbing Down* (Grand Rapids: Wm. B. Eerdmans Publishing Co., 1995), 72.

173. 2 Samuel 6:14–15.

174. 2 Samuel 6:21–22.

175. Annie Dillard, *Teaching a Stone to Talk* (New York: HarperCollins Publishers, 1982), 52.

176. Marva Dawn, *Reaching Out*, 206.

177. Hebrews 12:18a, 22–24.

178. Richard Caemmerer, *Preaching for the Church* (St. Louis: Concordia Publishing House, 1959), 51.

Chapter Twelve

179. Matthew 14:19 ESV.

180. Jon Acuff, "Traveling Mercies," *Stuff Christians Like*, blog, May 1, 2008, www.jonacuff.com/stuffchristianslike/2008/05/194-traveling-mercies/

181. James 4:2 NASB.

182. Lines attributed to Susanna Wesley.

183. Steve McVey, *52 Lies Heard in Church Every Sunday* (Eugene, OR: Harvest House Publishers, 2011), 81–82.

184. Ibid., 81.

185. 1 Thessalonians 5:18.

186. 1 Thessalonians 4:3.

187. Romans 12:2.

188. 1 Samuel 14:2.

189. 1 Samuel 14:6.

190. Erwin McManus, "Seizing Your Divine Moment," sermon transcript, *Preaching Today*, issue 252.

191. Erwin McManus, *An Unstoppable Force* (Loveland, CO: Group Publishing, 2001), 32–33.

192. 1 Samuel 14:6.

193. 1 Samuel 14:7.

194. 1 Samuel 14:8–10.

195. McManus, "Seizing Your Divine Moment."

196. 1 Samuel 14:11–12.

197. 1 Samuel 14:13–15.

198. McVey, *52 Lies*, 84.

A Final Word

199. 3 John 1:2.

200. Ephesians 3:19b.

201. Colossians 1:10b–11a.

"The Scandal of God's Love"

from Bob Hostetler's upcoming book,

How to Fall in Love with God

Not long ago, a small group leader in my church related the story of an evening when he, his wife, and their small group were talking about the life of faith, and someone used the phrase "falling in love with God." A few moments later, someone else said something similar, and still another added a mention of being "in love" with God.

The conversation broadened and deepened over the next few moments, until Melissa, a young mother in the group who usually listened and smiled without saying much, finally summoned all her courage.

"What are you guys talking about?" she asked. "What do you mean, 'fall in love with God?'"

The room fell silent.

A few of them looked around at each other. Some stared at the ceiling. Or the floor.

But no one had an answer.

Believe it or not, that's not unusual.

Some people talk about falling in love with God. And some people—perhaps the majority—have no idea what they're talking about. It's not uncommon for me to talk about being in love with God and see the person I'm talking to tilt his head to one side like a robin listening for the first worm of spring. Sometimes he'll let me keep talking, but sometimes he'll stop me to ask, "What are you talking about?" And some are even so bold as to press me for information, asking, "How's that work? How does a person fall in love with God?"

How *does* that work? How does a person fall in love with God? For some people, it seems to just happen; they never had to think much about it. But others can't imagine what kind of person would speak in those terms, or what kind of experience they're referring to. Is it a mystical kind of thing? Is it reserved only for the superspiritual? Or the lunatic fringe? Or can anyone do it? And why would anyone want to?

That's what this book is about.

Why Fall in Love with God?

It was a fragrant June day when I first asked the lovely Robin Wright to go out with me. I was fifteen. She was fifteen. We were both on the staff of a Christian camp near Cincinnati, Ohio. She was far and away the loveliest creature I had ever seen: tall, tanned, lithe, with brown hair that cascaded to her waist. I threw caution to the wind and asked her out. She turned me down, explaining that someone else had already asked her.

She dated that "someone else" for the rest of the summer. The next summer, I played it cool. I didn't ask her out. But I also barely let her out of my sight. After a few evenings of "hanging out" together, she pointed out that while we were spending large chunks of time with each other, I had never officially asked her out. So I did. And she said yes.

I don't know how long it took. I don't know just when it happened. But at some point, my teenage infatuation (and hormonal impulses) turned undeniably into love. At some point, I told her I loved her, and she said she loved me, too. After dating for two years, I asked her to marry me, and she said yes. Three years after our first date, when we were both incredibly mature nineteen-year-olds, we became husband and wife.

Why did I fall in love? Because she was beautiful, of course. And charming. And intelligent. But there was more to it than that. I wanted to fall in love. I wanted her to fall in love with me. I wanted us to be in love together.

But again—why? Why did I *want* to fall in love? Why does *anyone* want to fall in love?

Some might say we fall in love because we are biologically driven to reproduce ourselves, to propagate the human species. Others might suggest we fall in love because we seek self-actualization, the fulfillment of our maximum potential. Could be. But I think answer is a lot simpler than either of those reasons.

I think we want to fall in love because we instinctively sense—or perhaps know—that love is the most pleasurable of all human sensations. Love makes us feel good. Love makes us happy. Love satisfies our deepest needs.

That has been my experience, not only in my relationship with my wife, the lovely Robin, but also in my relationship with God. I want to fall in love with God for the same reason I wanted to fall in love with Robin: it is fulfilling. It is pleasurable. It rocks me like a hurricane. And it's not just me. It does the same for anyone.

It will do the same for you.

Retracing the Route

When Melissa asked that bold, honest question in her small group gathering, the other people in the room were stymied momentarily, but not because they didn't know anything about loving God. On the contrary, some of the people in her small group had been lovers of God for decades.

Back in the days before Garmin or other GPS device makers, I would usually obtain something called a TripTik from AAA travel services anytime I prepared for a long trip in my car. It was a handy, user-friendly tool for finding my way from here to there. But once the trip was over and I'd returned home, the TripTik went in the garbage. Once I made the trip, I didn't need to remember the route I took to get there.

I think that's pretty much how we tend to treat our spiritual journeys. Those of us who have fallen in love with God seldom save the directions. So if someone asks us, "How do you fall in love with God?" we suddenly realize that we don't remember the route we took to get there.

But someone has. His name was Hosea. He lived roughly three thousand years ago. He became something of an expert on falling in love with God. And his TripTik has been preserved for us in the ancient book of the Bible that bears his name.

The story of Hosea is one of the oldest—and most offbeat—romances in the history of literature. And it is all the more fascinating because it so happens that this fascinating book was intended to explain—first for Hosea and then for Israel—what Melissa was asking. It is a true-life account of how to fall in love with God.

A Fractured Fairy Tale

Let's set the stage. Like the scrolling screen that introduced the movie *Star Wars*, the story of Hosea begins with a sort of preamble:

"God spoke to a man named Hosea, the son of Beeri, back during the reigns of Uzziah, Jotham, Ahaz, and Hezekiah in Judah, and during the reign of Jeroboam the son of Joash, who was king in Israel" (Hosea 1:1, author's paraphrase).

That short introduction gives us the context, the setting for all that follows.

Hosea lived in the northern kingdom of Israel in the eighth century before the birth of Jesus. The descendants of Abraham, Isaac, and Jacob had for centuries been split into a northern kingdom, Israel, and a southern kingdom, Judah.

Judah, depending on which king was leading it at the time, had sometimes followed God and sometimes not.

The northern kingdom, Israel—which couldn't claim a single righteous king in all its years of existence—had been following a spiraling path deeper and deeper into sin.

So let's follow the story, because it will reveal the secret of falling in love with God. The story goes on:

"When Yahweh first began speaking through Hosea, he told him, 'I want you to go and find a whore. Marry her and have children with her, to demonstrate what my people have done by forsaking Yahweh'" (Hosea 1:2, author's paraphrase).

Once upon a time in a kingdom far, far away, God told a man named Hosea to find a whore and marry her. Not much of a fairy tale, is it?

Can you *imagine*? I mean, it's something to hear from God at all. But can you imagine hearing God say, "Go, look up the sleaziest woman you can find and get hitched"?

In fact, in some Bible translations, it's easy to miss the utterly shocking nature of God's words. But a few versions get closer to the impact of the original language:

> *"Go and marry a harlot"* (Phillips)
> *"Go and marry a prostitute"* (NLT)
> *"Find a whore and marry her"* (*The Message*)

Oh my. Oh my.

What would *you* do? I mean, God is God, right? When he says, "Jump," I'm supposed to say, "How high?"—especially if I'm a prophet. But still, dude! That's harsh!

I have to wonder if there are parts of the story that ended up, like many film scenes, on the cutting room floor. You know, was Hosea's first response, "Say what?" Or, "Come again?" Did Hosea have a mother to explain things to? Or a girlfriend? We don't know. We're not told. The Bible simply says next,

> *"So Hosea did just that. He went and found Gomer, the daughter of Diblaim. He married her, and she got pregnant by him and gave him a son"* (Hosea 1:3, author's paraphrase).

Again, there are so many blanks I wish had been filled in for us. We don't know if Hosea strolled through the red-light district saying, "No . . . no . . . not her . . . not that one . . . YES!" Or if God specified Gomer. (And, by the way, if you're a baby boomer, you can just stop picturing Gomer Pyle. This Gomer probably looked nothing like Jim Nabors.)

We don't know if Hosea just walked up to some lady of the evening and said, "Hi, you don't know me, but God told me to marry you." (Guys, this is never a good pickup line.) We're not told if Hosea had to woo her, taking her out for drinks and a donkey race one night and dinner and a dance the next. We just don't know. It doesn't say.

But we do know that Hosea, a prophet of God, actually married a prostitute because God told him to. Why would God do that? Why would he give Hosea such a weird command? Great question. And the answer, though it will be a while yet before we can fully grasp it, is all about how to fall in love with God.

And Baby Makes Three

Poor Hosea. Other judges and prophets got to play the hero. Samson brought down the house. Nathan blew the whistle. Elijah rode a chariot of fire. But Hosea's prophetic career started with a really awkward wedding, one that was probably worse than the flakiest reality TV show.

And then, perhaps while he was still trying to figure out how to be a husband, Hosea became a father. Gomer got pregnant, gave birth to a son, and then,

> *"When the boy was born, Yahweh told Hosea, 'Name him Jezre'el (meaning "God will scatter"), for I will soon punish King Jehu and his royal house for the blood he shed in Jezre'el, and I will abolish the kingdom of Israel. I will break Israel's military power in the Valley of Jezre'el'"* (Hosea 1:4–5, author's paraphrase).

Now, in Hebrew culture, just like in Native American culture, parents gave their babies names that *meant* something. (In fact, Hosea's own name—the same name as Joshua before him and Jesus after him—meant "The Lord saves," or "The Lord is my salvation.") But here God tells Hosea to name his son Jezre'el, which meant, literally, "God scatters," but it had come to be a synonym for "castaway." "Unwanted." "Reject."

Poor kid.

You thought it was tough growing up with *your* name? Try growing up with the name "Reject."

There was a divine reason, however, for such an unfortunate name. God chose it as a way of warning Israel that their wicked leadership would soon be destroyed and the whole nation would soon be rejected because of their wickedness. But the drama is just beginning.

Yours, Mine, and Not Mine

The story continues in verses 6 through 9:

> *Sometime later, Gomer got pregnant again and gave birth to a daughter. And Yahweh told Hosea, "Name her Lo-Ruhamah (meaning 'Unloved'), for I am through showing love to Israel; I am done forgiving them. I will show love to Judah, and deliver them from their enemies—but when I do, I'll make it clear that neither firepower nor strategy has saved them, but only Yahweh, their God."*
>
> *When Gomer had weaned Lo-Ruhamah, she became pregnant again and had another child, a son. And Yahweh said, "Give him the name, Lo-Ammi (meaning, Not Mine), because Israel is not my people, and I am not your God."*

Notice what's happening here. Gomer has two more children. But the Bible uses different phrasing to refer to those two births. The second and third time around, it doesn't say that Gomer gave Hosea a child—simply that she became pregnant and had a child. *Gomer* does. But apparently not Hosea.

Jezre'el is his son. Lo-Ruhamah and Lo-Ammi, not so much.

Oh my. Can you imagine how Hosea felt?

Out of obedience to God, he had married this woman who was a *prostitute* and perhaps—judging from her name, which means "consummate"—the worst of the worst, the whorest of the whores, so to speak. She was No One. She had nothing. And Hosea took her home and took her in, made her his wife, and bestowed his name on her. And she betrayed him in the worst possible way.

And not once.

It wasn't a mistake, a moment of weakness. It wasn't a fleeting lapse in judgment.

He had made her a bride . . . but she had made him a cuckold, a fool.

So God tells Hosea to name the children Lo-Ruhamah, or unloved, and Lo-Ammi, not my child, names that drive home not only the tragic results of Gomer's unfaithfulness to Hosea, but also of Israel's unfaithfulness to God.

It's a story we could call *The Prophet and the Prostitute*, a story of heartbreak, betrayal, and agony. It's a story that makes us ask again, "Why?" Why would God ask such things of poor Hosea? Why would he command this poor man to take a prostitute for a wife? Why would he tell him to give such awful names to his poor children? Why would he let Hosea suffer such undeserving heartbreak?

If you can understand the answer to that, you can start to trace the route to falling in love with God. Why did God ask such things of Hosea? So he would understand—not only in his head, but also in his heart, in his *gut*, through his own experience, the scandal of God's love for him, for Israel, for you.

Because, you see, one key to falling in love with God is *experiencing* the scandal of God's love for you. God didn't ask Hosea to proclaim his love, to prophesy his love, until Hosea had tasted on a human scale what it means to say . . .

God condescended to me in spite of my shame.

God told Hosea to go and marry a whore.

Can you even imagine what that was like? For Hosea to leave his cozy suburban bungalow to go to the seedy, sleazy red-light district, to a woman who had slept with three men the night before . . . and in the light of day, with mocking eyes watching, ask her to be his wife?

Can you imagine? This is no pretty scene out of a Julia Roberts movie. Only the ugliest, most sordid, most revolting, and most shameful condescension imaginable could even begin to put Hosea's heart in touch with the inconceivable distance between God's holiness and their filthiness. Only something that dramatic could demonstrate how far Yahweh would condescend, what he would do, for his bride. For me. For you.

Do you remember the story an early Christ-follower recorded, of the woman who had been caught in adultery and was dragged in front of Jesus so his enemies could use her to trap him?

Do you remember that after he confounded them by saying simply, "If any one of you is without sin, let him be the first to throw a stone at her," they all left, one by one?

And do you remember that when they were all gone and this adulterous woman was left alone with him, he said,

> *"Woman, where are they? Has no one condemned you?"*
>
> *"No one, sir," she said.*
>
> *"Then neither do I condemn you," Jesus declared. "Go now and leave your life of sin." (John 8:10–11)*

Do you know that he addressed her with the same term of respect he used with his own mother?

"Woman . . ."

"Ma'am . . ."

Do you know how far God condescended to be able to speak terms of love and respect . . . to you?

Do you know that he set aside majesty and glory, riches and comfort to be able to say,

> *"There is . . . no condemnation for those who are in Christ Jesus"* (Rom. 8:1).

Do you know that the amount of condescension involved in the infinite, eternal God entering time and space for *you* is *immeasurable*?

Do you know that he comes to you even in your shame?

Do you know that no matter how low you may feel, you're not too low for him to reach?

The psalmist said,

> *"If I make my bed in the depths, you are there"* (Ps. 139:8a).

Oh, the depth of the mercy of God! That he would condescend to you—to me—no matter how low we go, no matter how shameful we may feel, that he would condescend so far to us that Hosea had to marry a prostitute to even begin to grasp it.

Not only that, but Hosea's experience also shows us the scandal of God's love, in that . . .

God chose me in spite of my past.

My wife, the lovely Robin, is a fan of westerns. They don't even have to be good. So when the Kevin Costner movie *Open Range* came out, I took her to see it. Costner plays a hard-case, "free range" cowboy, who meets a woman, a doctor's sister, and they're taken with each other. But Costner's character holds back. He seems almost afraid of her. And at one point he reveals why: he's afraid if she knew his past she would be scared, disgusted, repulsed. It's clear his past is ugly, violent, vile.

When you've got a lot of garbage in your past, it's hard to believe someone would choose you. That's what victims of rape, abuse, and addiction struggle with. They find it hard to believe someone could ever choose them if that person knew all there was to know.

That was what happened when Hosea married Gomer, the daughter of Diblaim. The Bible doesn't tell us, but if I had to guess, I'd say Hosea probably chose the worst of the worst—no *Pretty Woman*, not at all—but the woman with the worst reputation, the worst past (which, as I said a few pages back, would have been in keeping with her name). Because only by doing that could God put Hosea's heart in touch with what God would do for me, with what God would do for you, when he chose you in spite of your past.

Paul the great church planter once wrote to the church in Corinth:

Do you not know that the wicked will not inherit the kingdom of God? Do not be deceived: Neither the sexually immoral nor idolaters nor adulterers nor male prostitutes nor homosexual offenders nor thieves nor the greedy nor drunkards nor slanderers nor swindlers will inherit the kingdom of God. And that is what some of you were. But you were washed, you were sanctified, you were justified in the name of the Lord Jesus Christ and by the Spirit of our God. (1 Cor. 6:9–11)

Oh, if you and I could fully realize that, despite our past—despite the abuse we suffered, despite the self-loathing we felt, despite the crummy choices we made, despite our sin, despite the family we had, despite our failures and flaws—God in Christ chose us. "You did not choose me," Jesus said, "but I chose you" (John 15:16).

We talk about choosing Christ. We sing, "I have decided to follow Jesus," and that's certainly how it looks from our perspective. But from the Bible's perspective—and from Hosea's perspective—it looks more like this:

> *You were dead in your transgressions and sins . . . gratifying the cravings of [your] sinful nature and following its desires and thoughts. . . .*
>
> *But because of his great love for [you], God, who is rich in mercy, made [you] alive with Christ even when [you] were dead in transgressions—it is by grace you have been saved.* (Eph. 2:1–2, 4–5)

Getting into Hosea's story ought to prompt us to fall in love with God, who is rich in mercy and abounding in grace toward us, as we realize his unfathomable, immeasurable condescension to find us and save us and make us his Bride.

And, finally, Hosea's experience also shows us the scandal of God's love in that . . .

God loves me in spite of my betrayal.

The Bible talks about "how wide and long and high and deep is the love of Christ" (Eph. 3:18). It's a poetic phrase. A beautiful image. But just how deep *is* the love of Christ?

This deep: Remember Lo-Ruhamah and Lo-Ammi? Hosea had to experience what it was like to watch his wife bear another man's children, to taste that bitter betrayal, *and love her anyway* in order to begin to understand how deep is the love of God.

It's this deep: Remember Judas? Jesus knew when he ate his last supper in the Upper Room with his followers that Judas had already betrayed him. But rather than expose him or banish him, Jesus washed his feet and dipped a piece of bread in the bowl of oil and herbs and gave it to Judas, a sign of hospitality and friendship that persists even to this day in Eastern lands.

It's this deep: Remember Peter? On the last night of his life, Jesus warned that Peter would deny him before the next morning, and Peter did ... vehemently. But when Jesus rose from the dead and appeared to Peter and the other disciples, he cooked him breakfast one morning by the sea and communicated his widelonghighdeep love by giving Peter a chance to renew his love for Jesus as many times as he had earlier denied it.

Of course, Judas hung himself, and so missed that kind of forgiveness and restoration. Ever wonder why? Why two men betrayed Jesus' love for them but one let his betrayal destroy him while the other found forgiveness and restoration?

I have a guess. Maybe it was so we can see the contrast ... and be warned by it.

Oh, I don't know about you, but I have many times betrayed God's love for me, no less than a wife who bears another man's child.

I have slept with the Enemy.

I have eaten at God's table and then moments later betrayed him as boldly as Judas.

I have failed him by the fires of unbelievers no less than Peter.

And I'm tempted to run from him like Judas—and so condemn myself. But if, instead, like Peter I throw off my outer garment, shed my inhibitions and baggage, and race to my waiting Savior, I will find not rejection but reconciliation, mercy, grace, and love.

The Rest of the Story

In spite of all the unfaithfulness and betrayal and spiritual adultery of Israel, the first chapter of Hosea concludes with a striking promise:

Still [God says], there will come a day when the people of Israel will be as numerous as sands on the seashore. In the very place where they were named, "Not Mine," they will be called, "God's Own." And the people of Judah and of Israel will be reunited, as one, under One. What a day of rejoicing that will be, a day of exaltation, the day of Jezre'el. (Hosea 1:10–11, author's paraphrase)

Through his obliging prophet Hosea, God promises to these people who had betrayed him like an adulterous wife that there will nonetheless come a day when *Lo-Ammi*—Not Mine—will become *bar El chai*—God's Own (literally, "sons of the Living God").

That's the kind of God you can fall in love with. If you, like Hosea, can somehow grasp that he condescended to you in spite of your shame, that he chose you in spite of your past, and that he loves you unconditionally in spite of your betrayal, then you may be on your way. If you can let the scandal of God's love for you enter into your heart and not only your head, then you may soon—perhaps before finishing this book—find yourself falling head over heels in love with God.

~§ Prayer

God, you really did condescend to me, didn't you? You chose me. You love me unconditionally. In spite of anything and everything, Lord, you care so much for me that you had your prophet Hosea marry a prostitute to show how wide and long and high and deep your love is for me.

It's hard to really feel "in touch" with that kind of love. But if you'll help me, God, I would like to understand—not only in my head, but in my heart, in my gut, through my own experience, the splendid and terrible scandal of your love for me. Amen.